For Jonas

Acknowledgments

I would like to thank Idelle Pandolfini for her creative assistance and editing; Larry Tamarkin for his production of the diagrams; Carol Ann Caronia for her thoughtful advice; Chess Master Bruce Alberston for his expertise and critical judgment; and Manhattan Chess Club technical assistants Chess Master Bruce Bowyer, International Arbiter Sophia Gorman, Jim Duggan, Steve Immitt, Mark Levine, Alan Reider, Chris Showers, Torrey Paulson, Roane Carey, Debra Bergman, and Charles Rue Woods for his direction and vision.

About This Book

This book contains 101 of Bobby Fischer's most brilliant, creative, daring, surprising, ingenious, eye-opening, revolutionary—or in one word—*outrageous* moves! They have been selected from all his recorded games, most of them played under tournament or match conditions.

For each of these situations, the setting and Fischer's opponent are designated at the top of the page, along with the impending move number. There follows on each page an outrageous move that occurred at a critical turning point in the game—a move that made all the difference. A diagram shows the position just before Fischer made his decisive play.

The reader is encouraged to guess Fischer's move on the basis of the accompanying clue. The solution for each is supplied at the bottom of the page, and in all cases the reasons for the move are explained in both words and algebraic notation, the contemporary standard. At the top right of each page, you'll find a shaded number that indicates the degree of difficulty, with 5 being the most difficult.

You can solve these positions by looking at the diagrams or by setting them up on your own board. They provide a detailed insight into the mind of a very great chessplayer, and as a source of entertainment, they're *outrageous* fun!

About Bobby Fischer

Robert James "Bobby" Fischer, generally acknowledged as the greatest chessplayer of all time, emerged on earth in Chicago, Illinois, March 9, 1943. His family later moved to Brooklyn, New York, where in 1949 he was introduced to the game by his eleven-year-old sister Joan, using the directions that came with the set.

Less than two years later, Bobby's mother sent a postcard to the *Brooklyn Eagle* newspaper inquiring about places to play chess. The card was answered by journalist Herman Helms, who alerted Mrs. Fischer to a chess exhibition planned for Brooklyn's Grand Army Plaza Library on January 17, 1951. Bobby played and lost that day to master Max Pavey, but he gained a chess teacher: Carmine Nigro, president of the Brooklyn Chess Club. Thereafter, Bobby played at the Brooklyn club Friday evenings and at Mr. Nigro's home on weekends. Sometimes his mentor even took the talented junior to Washington Square Park in Greenwich Village, where they played all day long.

Bobby participated in his first tournament, the 1955 U.S. Amateur, in upstate New York (receiving a minus score), and later that year joined the fiercely competitive Manhattan Chess Club. The Manhattan has "the strongest players of any club in the country," he wrote in his first book, *Bobby Fischer's Games of Chess* (Simon and Schuster, 1958). Starting off with players of average strength, he quickly moved up to the "B" group and then to the "A." And in the spring of 1956 came his first real tournament success, when he tied for first in the Manhattan Chess Club's "A" Reserve section.

This was the launching pad for his meteoric rise. Bobby then won the 1956 U.S. Junior Championship in Philadelphia, tied for 4th in the U.S. Open in Oklahoma City, and for 8th in Montreal's First Canadian Open (actually stronger than its

U.S. counterpart). His most memorable accomplishment in 1956 may well have been in the Rosenwald Trophy Tournament held at New York City's Manhattan and Marshall chess clubs, where thirteen-year-old Bobby finished in 8th place overall. But it was his truly inspired game against International Master Donald Byrne that received worldwide praise and was dubbed "the game of the century." The winning moves were perhaps the most insightful ever played by a youngster.

Even greater success lay ahead for the youthful whirlwind in 1957. He won the U.S. Junior Championship, the U.S. Junior Speed Championship, a match against Philippine Junior Champ Rodolfo Cardoso, and the New Jersey State Open. But the crown jewel came at year's end when, playing in his first Invitational U.S. Championship, Bobby overtook the famous Samuel Reshevsky and won first prize. At fourteen, Bobby Fischer had become the youngest U.S. Champion ever.

Subsequent achievements include:

- Becoming the youngest grandmaster in history at age fifteen in 1958.
- Going undefeated and capturing first prize in the 1962 Stockholm Interzonal Tournament.
- Winning the U.S. Championship all eight times he played, including an 11-0 blitz of the 1963-64 field, the first and only time it's ever been done.
- Demolishing ex-world champion Tigran Petrosian 3-1 (2 wins, 2 draws) in the 1970 USSR vs the Rest-of-the-World Match.
- Overwhelming the field by an unprecedented 5½ points in the 1970 World Speed Championship in Yugoslavia.
- Winning the 1970 Interzonal Tournament in Palma de Mallorca by 3½ points over his nearest rival.
- Destroying consecutively three top grandmasters in the 1971 Candidates Matches: Russia's Mark Taimanov 6-0; Denmark's Bent Larsen 6-0 (the first two such shutouts ever); and the Soviet Union's Petrosian 6½-2½ winning the final four games.
- Defeating in 1972 at Reykjavik, Iceland, his long-time

nemesis, Russia's Boris Spassky, in the greatest chess match of all time, to become America's first and only World Champion.

Bobby's hiatuses from competitive chess from 1964 to 1970 stemmed from various disagreements with chess organizers over rules, conditions, and prizes. His triumph in the 1970 USSR vs the Rest-of-the-World Match signaled his return, climaxed by his incredible 1972 victory over Spassky. In 1975, when he disputed the World Chess Federation's championship rules for a match against the Soviet player Anatoli Karpov, he declined to compete and Karpov was given the title without ever having faced Fischer across the board.

Still, much of the world continued to regard Fischer as the undethroned chess champ, a unique circumstance in that he eschewed tournament and match play thereafter. In fact, when he chose to play MIT's Greenblatt Computer chess program in 1978 (which he beat three times to none), he made no attempt to publicize the encounter and even tried to keep it private. This, of course, was impossible, for Fischer had achieved the status of folk hero.

Beyond the endless puzzlement and speculation about Fischer's future intentions in chess, there is one certainty: his games will live forever. There are one hundred and one of his virtuoso tactics in this book. They are a thing of beauty and sufficient reason for reading on.

About Algebraic Notation

Algebraic notation is the clearest way to describe chess moves, using letters **a** to **h** and numbers **1** to **8**. It's also the officially recognized notational system of both the world and U.S. chess federations (FIDE and USCF, respectively).

The chessboard itself is an 8-by-8 grid, with vertical rows called *files* and horizontal rows called *ranks*. Letters signify files, numbers designate ranks.

Each square is named by its intersecting letter and number as in diagram A. In diagram B, White's King occupies b6; White's Bishops d7 and e7; and Black's King b8. All squares are always named from White's point of view.

Symbols You Should Know

K means King
Q means Queen
R means Rook
B means Bishop
N means Knight (so as not to confuse with the King)
Pawns are not symbolized (they are named by the letter of the file occupied—the pawn on the b-file is the b-pawn)
x means captures
+ means check
0-0 means castles Kingside
0-0-0 means castles Queenside
! means very good move
!! means brilliant move
? means questionable move
?? means blunder
1. means White's first move
1 . . . means Black's first move

(1-0) means White wins
(0-1) means Black wins

Reading the Line Score of a Game

Consider diagram B. White to play could mate in two moves and it would be written this way.

1. Bd6+ Ka8 2. Bc6 mate.
1. Bd6+ means that White's first move was Bishop to d6 check.
Ka8 means that Black's first move was King to a8.
2. Bc6 mate means that White's second move was Bishop to c6 checkmate.

Note that the number of the move is written only once, appearing just before White's play. For the examples in the book, the actual moves Fischer and his opponent played are given in **boldface** type. Interesting possibilities that were not played are given in regular type.

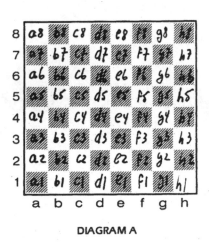

DIAGRAM A

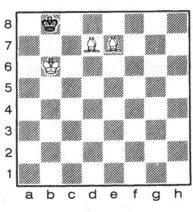

DIAGRAM B

Bobby Fischer vs Bent Larsen

DENVER, 1971
5TH MATCH GAME
WHITE'S 43RD MOVE

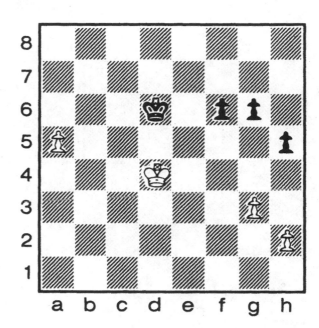

CLUE: Both sides have equal material, but Fischer's outside passed pawn, along with his more centralized King, makes all the difference.

SOLUTION: Fischer played **1. a6!**, trying to decoy Black's King from the Kingside. After **1 . . . Kc6 2. a7 Kb7 3. Kd5 h4**, Larsen is hoping that White accepts doubled h-pawns by 4. gxh4. Instead, **4. Ke6** and Larsen resigned. His remaining pawns must fall to Fischer's marauding King. **(1-0)**

Bobby Fischer vs William Addison

CLEVELAND, 1957
U.S. OPEN
WHITE'S 29TH MOVE

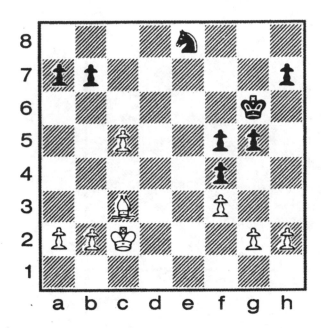

CLUE: In effect, Fischer has an extra c-pawn, for Black's Kingside majority is crippled by White's three pawns. Another advantage: White has a powerful Bishop against an inferior Knight, allowing Fischer to reduce the position to bare essentials.

SOLUTION: Fischer played **1. Be5!**, corraling the Knight so that it can't move without being captured. On either 1 . . . Ng7 or 1 . . . Nf6, White swaps the Bishop for the Knight and arrives at a winning King and pawn endgame, where his Queenside pawn majority decides. The game concluded: **1 . . . Kh5 2. Kd3 g4 3. b4 a6 4. a4 gxf3 5. gxf3 Kh4 6. b5 axb5 7. a5! Kh3 8. c6**, and Black resigned, for after 8 . . . bxc6 the a-pawn moves up the board unhampered while Black's Knight sits by helplessly. **(1-0)**

Bobby Fischer vs Luis Sanchez

SANTIAGO, 1959
WHITE'S 53RD MOVE

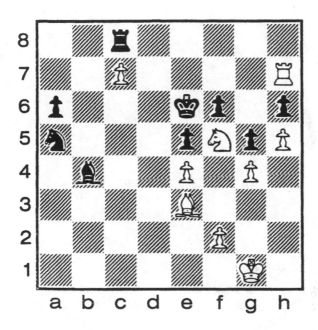

CLUE: White's assets include a far-advanced passed pawn and harmoniously working pieces. Black's are disorganized. Add to Black's woes that his Bishop is tied up defending against Re7 mate—the crux of the problem.

SOLUTION: White scored with 1. **Bd2!**. Fischer's Bishop cannot be captured because of his mate threat at e7. Defending Black's Bishop with 1 . . . Nc6 fails to 2. Bxb4, and if Sanchez recaptures he's again mated at e7. Finally, if he saves his Bishop by moving it off the a5-e1 diagonal, he hangs his Knight at a5. Black resigned. **(1-0)**

Bobby Fischer vs Joaquim Durao

HAVANA, 1966
17TH OLYMPIAD
WHITE'S 33RD MOVE

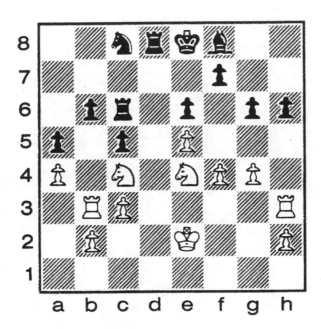

CLUE: Black hasn't lost anything yet, though four of his five pieces are in defensive positions along the back rank. This bodes ill, and Fischer capitalized at once.

SOLUTION: Fischer converted his spatial edge into winning a pawn by **1. Nxa5!**, when 1 . . . bxa5 allows 2. Nf6+ Ke7 3. Rb7+ and mate in two moves (Black can temporarily save his King by discarding both Rooks). Black declined the sacrifice with **1 . . . Rc7**, accepting a pawn-down endgame, which he soon abandoned. **(1-0)**

Bobby Fischer vs Tigran Petrosian

BLED, YUGOSLAVIA 1961
ALEKHINE MEMORIAL TOURNAMENT
WHITE'S 36TH MOVE

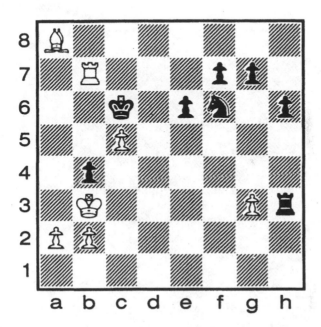

CLUE: Black's King has just played to c6, blundering into a potential discovered attack from the Bishop. White has merely to move his Rook and it's check, but where? Fischer uncorks the answer.

SOLUTION: Actually, White didn't start with a Rook move at all. Fischer first played the preparatory **1. Kc4!**, defending his c-pawn and constructing a mating net. Black resigned, unable to stop a subsequent Ra7 discovered mate. Fischer's outrageous King move brought the house down. **(1-0)**

Paul Keres vs Bobby Fischer

BLED, 1959
CANDIDATES TOURNAMENT
BLACK'S 53RD MOVE

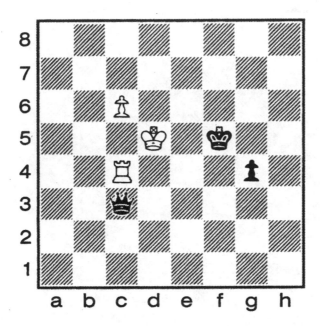

CLUE: Keres has just played his Rook to c4, attacking Black's Queen, but blocking the last escape square for his own King. Fischer quickly knew what to do.

SOLUTION: The curtain was drawn with **1 . . . Qe5 mate**. This uncommon mating pattern is sometimes referred to as a swallow's-tail mate because the pieces are arranged somewhat like a bird in flight, with the c6 and c4 squares as the bird's wings. It was scandalous that Fischer actually thus checkmated one of the world's great grandmasters! **(0-1)**

Bobby Fischer vs Arthur Bisguier

POUGHKEEPSIE, 1963
NEW YORK STATE OPEN
WHITE'S 27TH MOVE

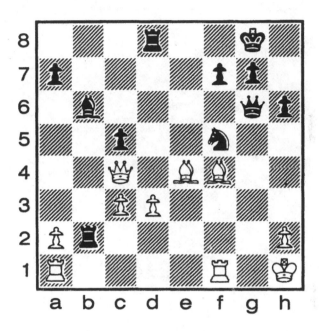

CLUE: With a Rook on the 7th rank and a Queen and Knight menacing White's Kingside, Black appears to have a dangerous position. But Fischer's centralized Bishops, poised for both defense and attack, save the day.

SOLUTION: "Knightfall" overtook Black after **1. Be5!**, when there was no way to avert the loss of the horseman pinned to his Queen by the Bishop at e4. The game concluded: **1 . . . Re8** (one move too late to guard e5) **2. Rxf5 Rxe5 3. Rxe5**, and Black resigned. **(1-0)**

Bobby Fischer vs E. Osbun

DAVIS, CALIFORNIA, 1964
SIMULTANEOUS EXHIBITION, WITH CLOCKS
WHITE'S 44TH MOVE

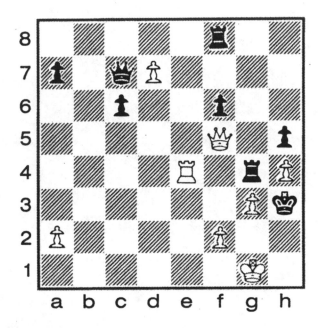

CLUE: Black has just shielded his King from White's Queen by interposing his Rook at g4. Black's reliance on this faulty defense is as "iffy" as the geological crack along the California coast, site of the matchup. It would have taken an eight-point earthquake on the Richter scale to stop Fischer's imminent mate.

SOLUTION: Fischer presciently exchanged Rooks **1. Rxg4!** **hxg4** and then surprisingly retreated his Queen **2. Qd3!**, threatening 3. Qf1 mate. With no reasonable way to extricate his King, Black gave up. **(1-0)**

Bobby Fischer vs Enrique Mecking

PALMA DE MALLORCA, SPAIN, 1970
INTERZONAL TOURNAMENT
WHITE'S 19TH MOVE

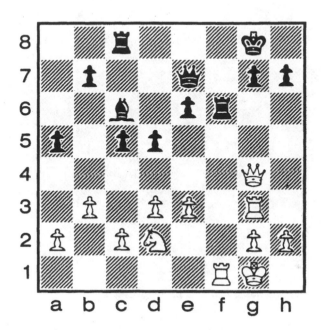

CLUE: White's Rooks and Queen loom down on Black, though all targets seem beyond White's scope. Bobby proved otherwise and won a pawn. How? Time will reveal all.

SOLUTION: After **1. Qxg7 + !** **Qxg7**, with Black's Queen pinned, White had the time for a mercenary *zwischenzug* (a German word for "in-between move") **2. Rxf6**, knowing Mecking's Queen couldn't escape capture anyway. A pawn to the good, Fischer nursed his advantage to win in 42 moves. **(1-0)**

Paul Keres vs Bobby Fischer

BLED, 1959
CANDIDATES TOURNAMENT
BLACK'S 24TH MOVE

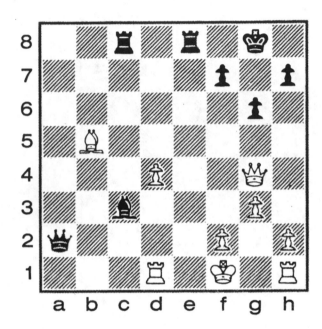

CLUE: White's Bishop at b5 attacks Black's Rook at e8. But Fischer's defense shows who the real attacker is.

SOLUTION: Fischer turned the tables with **1 . . . Qd5!**, attacking White's Bishop (b5) and Rook (h1) simultaneously. The play continued: **2. Bxe8 Qxh1 + 3. Ke2 Rxe8 +** (collecting his piece with check) **4. Kd3** (threatening Black's Queen and Bishop) **4 . . . Be1**, and Fischer remained a piece ahead, provoking White's resignation. **(0-1)**

Bobby Fischer vs Pal Benko

CURACAO, 1962
CANDIDATES TOURNAMENT
WHITE'S 31ST MOVE

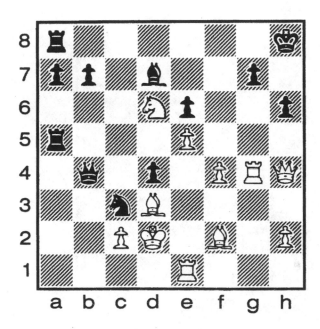

CLUE: White has two Bishops to Black's one. On the other side of the ledger are Black's pieces poised at the White King. It's White's turn, however, and Black could be mated before he can realize his attack.

SOLUTION: Fischer suddenly terminated Benko with **1. Qxh6 + !**. Mate next move follows by either 1 . . . gxh6 2. Nf7 or 1 . . . Kg8 2. Qxg7. **(1-0)**

Armando Acevedo vs Bobby Fischer

SIEGEN, WEST GERMANY, 1970
19TH OLYMPIAD
BLACK'S 47TH MOVE

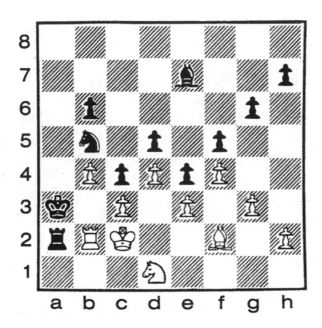

CLUE: White has an obstructed Bishop, a blocked Rook, and a lame Knight. His King isn't so safe either, but how can Fischer administer the death blow when everything is so impeded?

SOLUTION: The quickest road is **1. . . Nxc3!**, when 2. Nxc3? loses the Rook (2 . . . Rxb2+) and 2. Rxa2+ allows Black to extricate his Knight (2 . . . Nxa2). White tried **2. Kxc3** and resigned after the Knight-threatening **2. . .Ra1**. Neither 3. Kc2 Rxd1 4. Kxd1 Kxb2 nor 3. Rd2 Rc1+ 4. Rc2 Rxd1 offers any real resistance. **(0-1)**

Bobby Fischer vs Istvan Bilek

NEW YORK—HAVANA (BY TELETYPE), 1965
CAPABLANCA MEMORIAL TOURNAMENT
WHITE'S 35TH MOVE

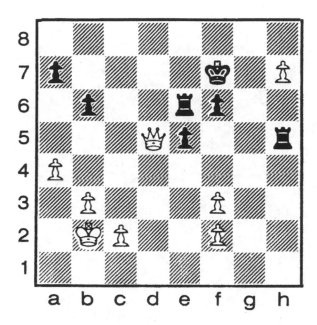

CLUE: It's a classic matchup: A Queen versus two Rooks. The Rooks are effective when they work in unison, but the Queen dominates when the Rooks are not coordinated and there are plenty of targets. Pawns can hinder, and pawns can help, as happens here.

SOLUTION: The humbling move was **1. f4!**, threatening the pinned Rook by 2. f5, when 2 . . . Rxf5 allows White's h-pawn to Queen. Note that another pin (along the 5th rank) prevents Black from playing 1 . . . exf4, which then hangs the Rook at h5 to White's Queen. Of course 1 . . . Rxh7 fails directly to 2. f5, winning the Rook at e6 outright. So the game continued: **1 . . . f5** (to prevent White's menacing advance) **2. fxe5 Rxh7 3. Qd7 + Re7 4. Qxf5 +** (giving White connected passed pawns on the e- and f-files) **4 . . . Ke8 5. f4 Kd8 6. e6**, and Black resigned. The marching pawns would only cost him more material. **(1-0)**

Bobby Fischer vs Julio Bolbochan

STOCKHOLM, 1962
INTERZONAL TOURNAMENT
WHITE'S 35TH MOVE

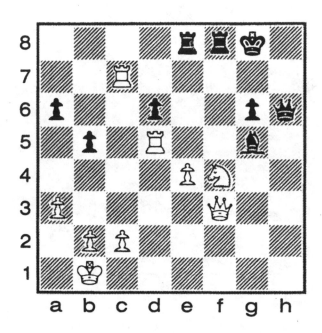

CLUE: It looks bad for White's Knight—pinned, attacked three times, and defended only once. Can the pin be broken?

SOLUTION: Yes. White's shift **1. Qb3!** not only undid the pin, but also set up a winning tactic—a discovered check along the a2-g8 diagonal by moving the Rook at d5. Black bit with **1 . . . Rxf4**. But after **2. Re5+** (somewhat stronger than 2. Rxg5+) **2 . . . Kf8** (to guard the Rook at e8) **3. Rxe8+**, Black resigned. The try 3 . . . Kxe8 allows mate after 4. Qe6+ Kf8 5. Qc8+. **(1-0)**

Bobby Fischer vs James Sherwin

NEW YORK, 1962-63
U.S. CHAMPIONSHIP
WHITE'S 26TH MOVE

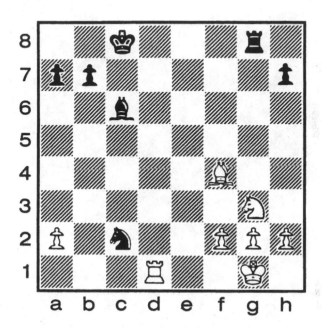

CLUE: If you focus on Black's Bishop and Rook, you might think they provide sufficient counterplay for being down a pawn. They will both ultimately converge on the square g2, where lies Fischer's moment of truth.

SOLUTION: Fischer played the subtly double-edged **1. Nf5!**. It certainly exposes the g-pawn, though it also threatens more seriously 2. Ne7 mate. With Black's Rook vulnerable to the Knight fork at e7, he tried 1 . . . **Rxg2 +**, but after **2. Kf1 b6 3. Ne7 + Kb7 4. Nxc6**, he couldn't take the Knight at c6 and at the same time save his Rook. Black played one more move **4 . . . Rg4** and resigned, for White can save his pieces by checking at d8 with his Knight and then moving his Bishop. **(1-0)**

Bobby Fischer vs Pal Benko

CURACAO, 1962
CANDIDATES TOURNAMENT
WHITE'S 31ST MOVE

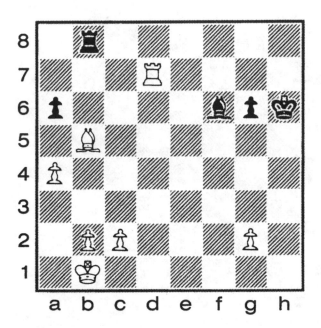

CLUE: Black is two pawns down, but with the Bishops operating on different colored squares, Fischer's opponent does have some drawing possibilities. Fischer calculated a powerful simplifying move.

SOLUTION: The most economical solution is **1. Rd6!**, hitting both the Bishop at f6 and the a-pawn. If Black moves his Bishop to safety, then White wins the a-pawn (2. Rxa6) and obtains a cluster of three Queenside pawns. The game concluded: **1 . . . Bxb2** (a desperate tactic, indirectly exchanging his Bishop for White's, capturing as much enemy material as he can in the process) **2. Kxb2 axb5 3. a5!** (producing a serious passed pawn) **3 . . . Ra8 4. a6 Kh5 5. Kb3 g5 6. Kb4 Kg4 7. Kxb5 Kg3 8. Rd7 g4 9. a7**, and Black resigned. On 9 . . . Kxg2, White follows through with 10. Kb6 and 11. Kb7, winning the Rook. **(1-0)**

Bobby Fischer vs William Addison

PALMA DE MALLORCA, 1970
INTERZONAL TOURNAMENT
WHITE'S 21ST MOVE

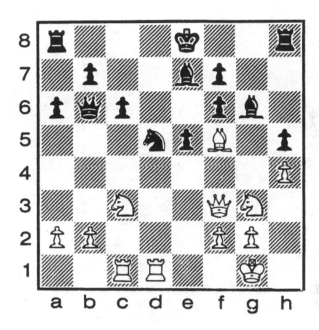

CLUE: White is fully developed and Black's King is still in the center. It won't be there for long, unless White drives home his initiative.

SOLUTION: Fischer controlled matters with **1. Rxd5!**, an exchange sacrifice. After the obligatory 1 . . . **cxd5 2. Nxd5**, White threatens Nc7, forking King and Rook. Addison avoided 2 . . . Qd8 for fear of 3. Bxg6 fxg6 4. Nc7+, when 4 . . . Kf7 is answered by 5. Qb3+, soon taking Black to the cleaners. The game continued: **2 . . . Qxb2 3. Rb1 Qxa2 4. Rxb7** and Black resigned. He had to cope with numerous threats, such as 5. Bxg6 fxg6 6. Nxf6+ Bxf6 7. Qxf6 leading to mate. **(1-0)**

Bobby Fischer vs Max Euwe

LEIPZIG, 1960
14TH OLYMPIAD
WHITE'S 36TH MOVE

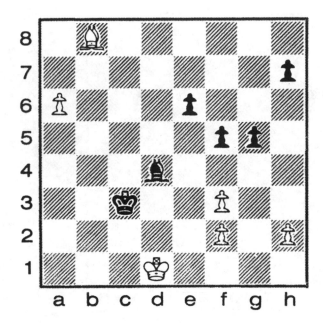

CLUE: White has a lusty passed pawn, but Black has some drawing chances if he can sacrifice his Bishop for the dangerous a-pawn. Fischer dispels the opportunity.

SOLUTION: The end came immediately with **1. Be5!**. This pinned the opposing Bishop and prevented it from guarding the a7 square. Thus, if 1 . . . Bxe5, then 2. a7 makes a new Queen. And if Black does anything else, White trades Bishops and pushes through his a-pawn. The great Dr. Euwe resigned. **(1-0)**

Svetozar Gligoric vs Bobby Fischer

PALMA DE MALLORCA, 1970
INTERZONAL TOURNAMENT
BLACK'S 29TH MOVE

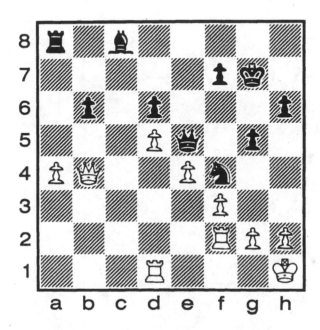

CLUE: Black has a Bishop and Knight in exchange for White's Rook and pawn. White's last move **Rf1-f2** enabled Fischer to exploit to the fullest his slight material edge.

SOLUTION: Fischer instantly saw that **1 . . . Nd3!**, forking the Queen and Rook, worked, for White's Rook at d1 couldn't leave the back rank to capture the Knight (2. Rxd3 allows 2 . . . Qa1 + and mate shortly). Gligoric fought on, only to resign after **2. Qxb6 Nxf2 + 3. Qxf2 Rxa4 4. Kg1 Ra1 5. Qe1 Ra2 6. Qg3 Qb2 7. h4 Ra1. (0-1)**

Donato Rivera vs Bobby Fischer

VARNA, BULGARIA, 1962
15TH OLYMPIAD
BLACK'S 14TH MOVE

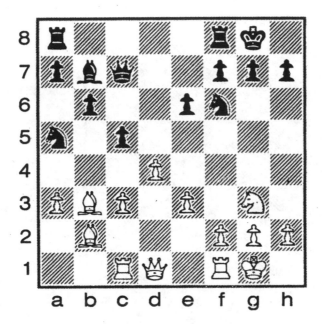

CLUE: White's last move, **1. Ra1-c1**, looked hunky-dory but was a mistake. Black now wins a decisive amount of material by shifting from a rank, to a diagonal, to a file.

SOLUTION: Fischer found **1 . . . Qc6!**, threatening diagonal mate at g2. This forced White to waste a move warding off the threat **2. f3**, which allowed **2 . . . Qb5**, skewering White's Bishops along the b-file. White tried one more move **3. Ba4**, and resigned after **3 . . . Qxb2**. (0-1)

Mark Taimanov vs Bobby Fischer

VANCOUVER, 1971
CANDIDATES MATCH 5th GAME
BLACK'S 46TH MOVE

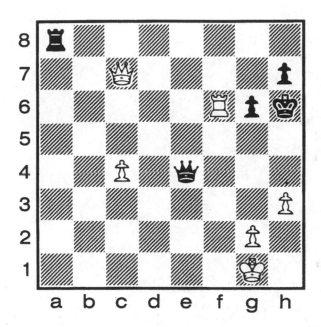

CLUE: What a blunder! How can a top grandmaster be provoked into playing a losing move like **Rf1xf6??**, throwing away an otherwise drawn position? Careful—it could happen to you!

SOLUTION: White was punished for his mistake by Fischer's **1 . . . Qd4+**, a Rook and King Fork. White conceded, for 2. Rf2 Ra1+ wins the Rook. And yet another grandmaster bites the dust! **(0-1)**

Bent Larsen vs Bobby Fischer

DENVER, 1971
CANDIDATES MATCH 2ND GAME
BLACK'S 37TH MOVE

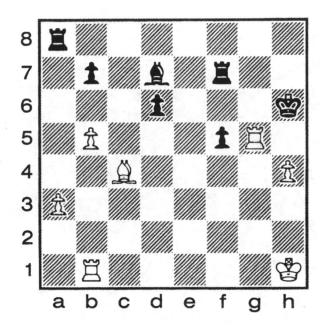

CLUE: White's threat: to capture the Rook at f7 with the Bishop. Is there a powerful countermove for Black's Rook in Fischer's bag of wizardry?

SOLUTION: Yes, there is: for the Rook at a8! Fischer took the offensive with **1 . . . Ra4!!**, when 2. Bxf7 Rxh4 + (shifting from one flank to the other) 3. Kg2 Kxg5 leaves Black a pawn ahead. Rather than accepting his state, Larsen compounded his problems with **2. Rc1?**, which dropped another pawn after **2 . . . Bxb5!**, for the pin along the 4th rank still exists. Fischer won the ensuing endgame with his usual immaculate technique. **(0-1)**

Bobby Fischer vs Jorge Rubinetti

BUENOS AIRES, 1970
WHITE'S 23RD MOVE

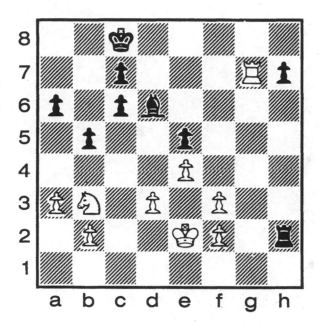

CLUE: It's a strange position. One Black pawn restrains four White ones. Can Fischer solve the mystery of this "Southern Cross" configuration?

SOLUTION: Since White's f-pawns are doubled anyway, he cleverly throws one away to free the others by **1. f4!**. After taking the pawn **1 . . . exf4**, Black was in severe trouble: **2. d4 Kd8 3. Na5 c5 4. e5 Bf8** (4 . . . Be7 loses a piece to 5. Nc6 +) **5. Nc6 + Ke8 6. Rxc7.** Rubinetti resigned. If he had continued 6 . . . cxd4, White pushes 7. e6, threatening the unstoppable 8. Rc8. **(1-0)**

Tigran Petrosian vs Bobby Fischer

BUENOS AIRES, 1971
CANDIDATES MATCH 6TH GAME
BLACK'S 59TH MOVE

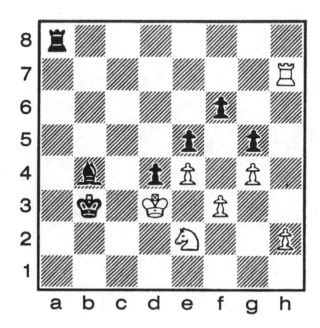

CLUE: A familiar story: Fischer has a Bishop against a Knight and a better-placed King. Throw in a menacing d-pawn and an aggressive Rook, and the White King is soon surrounded.

SOLUTION: Fischer's rapier-like **1 . . . Ra1!** threatens to envelop White's King (2 . . . Rd1 mate). With no recourse, White sacrificed his Knight **2. Nxd4+ exd4 3. Kxd4**, but after **3 . . . Rd1+** (so White's King can't meander to d5 and then e6) **4. Ke3 Bc5+ 5. Ke2 Rh1 6. h4** (on 6 . . . Rxh4 7. Rxh4 gxh4, White hopes to draw because Black's Bishop doesn't guard the h-pawn's Queening square h1) **6 . . . Kc4 7. h5 Rh2+ 8. Kel Kd3**, White resigned. If he had played 9. Kf1 (to avoid the back-rank mate) then 9 . . . Rf2+ eats more material. **(0-1)**

Bobby Fischer vs MIT's Greenblatt Computer Program

CAMBRIDGE, MASSACHUSETTS, 1978
WHITE'S 19TH MOVE

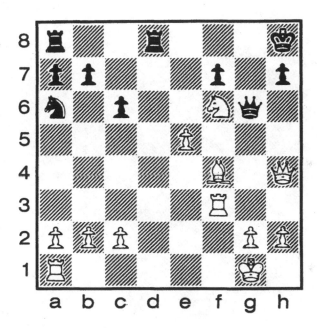

CLUE: When the chess community first heard about this stunt they questioned that it was really Fischer playing (since he hadn't publicly competed since 1972). But how could he resist the opportunity to ruthlessly pull the plug on an upstart robot?

SOLUTION: Fischer essayed the quietly powerful **1. Rc1!**. By guarding his c-pawn instead of moving it, White took away two important squares for Black's Queen to flee to along the c2-h7 diagonal. The computer never resigns, so after **1 . . . Kg7 2. Rg3 Rh8**, Fischer knocked its binary lights out with **3. Qh6** mate. Yes, 3. Bh6 is also mate. **(1-0)**

Bobby Fischer vs Tigran Petrosian

BUENOS AIRES, 1971
CANDIDATES MATCH 1ST GAME
WHITE'S 38TH MOVE

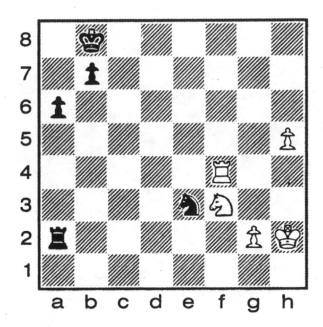

CLUE: If you're in a pawn race, better get off on the right foot. This race is not to the strong, but to the more centralized.

SOLUTION: Fischer stepped correctly with **1. Re4!**, so that 1 . . . Rxg2+ **2. Kh3** leaves two Black pieces attacked and clumsily placed. So Petrosian tried **1. Nxg2 2. Kg3** (note the Knight now has no safe move) **2 . . . Ra5 3. Ne5!** (a game-ending centralization). Since his pieces are unable to beat the h-pawn to the finish line, Black resigned. **(1-0)**

Bobby Fischer vs Milan Matulovic

HERCEG NOVI, YUGOSLAVIA, 1970
WORLD 5-MINUTE CHAMPIONSHIP
WHITE'S 31ST MOVE

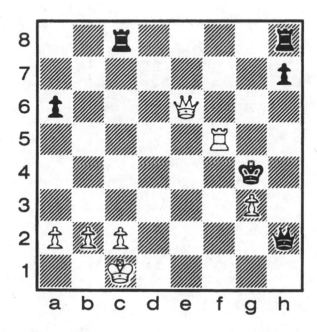

CLUE: Quick! This was a speed game, so answer the question fast. How can Fischer mate in three moves at most? Whew!

SOLUTION: Fischer expedited matters with **1. Rf4 + !**, and if 1 . . . Kg5 (or 1 . . . Kh5) then 2. Qg4 + Kh6 3. Rf6 mate. But Black found a more rapid way to lose, capturing the g-pawn with his King and allowing **2. Qg4 mate**. Not quite the Fool's Mate, but . . . **(1-0)**

Bobby Fischer vs Eugenio German

STOCKHOLM, 1962
INTERZONAL TOURNAMENT
WHITE'S 26TH MOVE

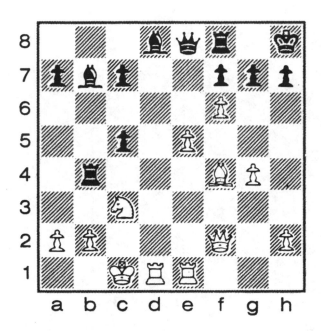

CLUE: White's Kingside offensive has beaten Black's Queen-side *Putsch* to the punch, but the knockout will require some fancy footwork.

SOLUTION: Fischer set up his one-two combination with **1. Bg5!**, threatening 2. Rxd8 and 3. fxg7 +, winning the Queen. Black tried to shield himself with **1 . . . Rd4**, but **2. fxg7 + Kxg7 3. Bf6 + Kg8** (3 . . . Bxf6 4. exf6 + uncovers a winning attack on Black's Queen) **4. Qh4** (threatening 5. Qg5 mate) **4 . . . Rxd1 + 5. Nxd1** (5. Rxd1?? permits the sucker punch 5 . . . Qxe5!, when 6. Bxe5 is met by 6 . . . Bxh4, regaining the Queen) and German resigned. If Black captures on f6 (5 . . . Bxf6), White threatens the Queen and mate with 6. exf6. **(1-0)**

Samuel Reshevsky vs Bobby Fischer

NEW YORK, 1963-64
U.S. CHAMPIONSHIP
BLACK'S 47TH MOVE

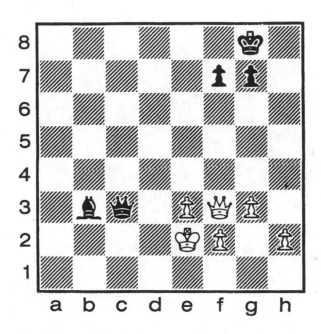

CLUE: White has two pawns against a Bishop, and he can give a few needling Queen checks, if he gets a free turn. That never happened.

SOLUTION: White expired after 1 . . . Qc4 + !. It's mate after 2. Kd2 Qc2 + 3. Kel Qc1 + 4. Ke2 Qd1. **(0-1)**

Bobby Fischer vs William Hook

SIEGEN, 1970
19TH OLYMPIAD
WHITE'S 28TH MOVE

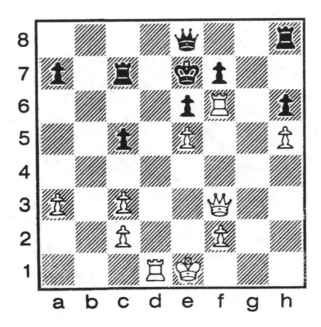

CLUE: White seems to have an inevitable mating attack, even against Black's well-defended pieces, if he can occupy a certain square.

SOLUTION: The clearing sacrifice **1. Rxe6 + !** threatens mate next move, in that either 1 . . . Kxe6 or 1 . . . fxe6 is answered by 2. Qf6 mate. 1 . . . Kf8 only leads to severe loss of material and certain loss of the game. **(1-0)**

Bobby Fischer vs Pal Benko

Bled, 1959
CANDIDATES TOURNAMENT
WHITE'S 39TH MOVE

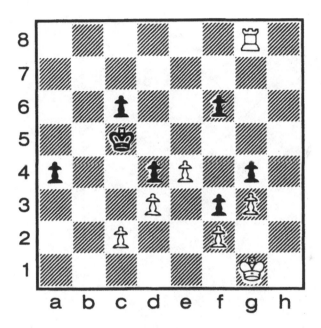

CLUE: White's a Rook ahead but Black's a-pawn may easily threaten to Queen, winning back the Rook. Fischer eviscerated it at once.

SOLUTION: The cutoff **1. Rb8!** stops the enemy King in its tracks. White now wins by moving his own King over to the Queenside. And if Black advances 1 . . . a3, then 2. Rb3 a2 3. Ra3 guts the a-pawn, so Benko resigned. **(1-0)**

Wolfgang Uhlmann vs Bobby Fischer

PALMA DE MALLORCA, 1970
INTERZONAL TOURNAMENT
BLACK'S 12TH MOVE

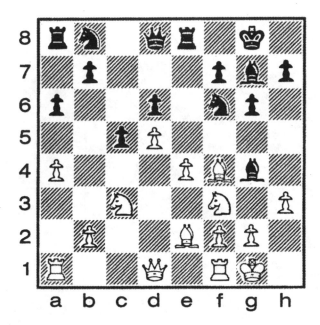

CLUE: Black's Bishop is attacked. Should he retreat it or capture the Knight on f3? Either one is hackneyed, right?

SOLUTION: Why reply in stereotypical fashion, capturing on f3 or retreating, when you can instead pilfer a pawn? Fischer played . . . **Nxe4!**, plucking a hapless foot soldier. As the analysis shows: 2. hxg4 Bxc3 3. bxc3 Nxc3 4. Qd2 Nxe2+ 5. Kh1 Nxf4 6. Qxf4 leaves Black two pawns ahead, and 2. Nxe4 Rxe4 3. hxg4 Rxf4 leaves Black a pawn ahead. Fischer, a master at bypassing quotidian play in favor of unearthing a hidden resource, won in 34 moves. **(0-1)**

Bobby Fischer vs Pal Benko

BLED, 1959
CANDIDATES TOURNAMENT
WHITE'S 18TH MOVE

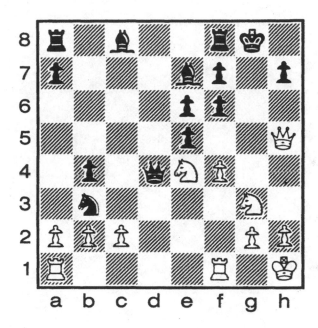

CLUE: Black's Knight has just captured White's Bishop (Nxb3). Standard principle suggests capturing toward the center (axb3) instead of away from the center (cxb3). So what else is new?

SOLUTION: If you followed the rule of thumb, you'd capture toward the center, that is, if you didn't have the stronger **1. Qh6!**, preparing 2. Nh5 and 3. Qg7 mate. Black answered 1 ... **exf4** (trying to clear the Queen's diagonal to g7), and the game went on: **2. Nh5 f5** (guarding against Qg7 mate) **3. Ra-d1** (still not taking on b3 so that he can gain a tempo by attacking the Queen) **3 ... Qe5** (keeping sentinel over g7 and preparing to sacrifice itself on f6) **4. Ne-f6+ Bxf6 5. Nxf6+ Qxf6 6. Qxf6 Nc5 7. Qg5+ Kh8 8. Qe7! Ba6 9. Qxc5 Bxf1 10. Rxf1** and Black gave up. **(1-0)**

Bobby Fischer vs Wolfgang Unzicker

SIEGEN, 1970
19TH OLYMPIAD
WHITE'S 36TH MOVE

3

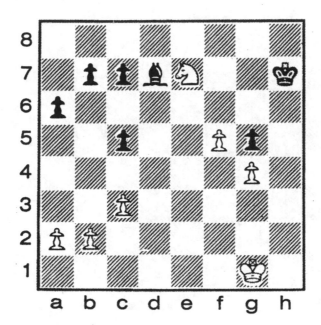

CLUE: White is practically a pawn ahead because of Black's doubled c-pawns. Though a Bishop is ordinarily a shade stronger than a Knight, White's steed can do some fancy prances to win and hold on to material.

SOLUTION: Fischer wins a pawn with **1. Nd5!**, zeroing in on the c-pawn and also threatening the fork 2. Nf6+. Play continued: **1 . . . Bc6 2. Nxc7 Bf3 3. Ne8!** (saving the g-pawn in that 3 . . . Bxg4 loses the Bishop to another fork, 4. Nf6+) **3 . . . Kh6 4. Nf6 Kg7 5. Kf2** (a useful in-between move bringing the King closer to the g-pawn) **5 . . . Bd1 6. Nd7 c4** (taking the g-pawn loses to 7. f6+ Kg8 8. f7+! Kxf7 9. Ne5+, winning the Bishop) **7. Kg3** and Black resigned. **(1-0)**

Victor Korchnoi vs Bobby Fischer

CURACAO, 1962
CANDIDATES TOURNAMENT
BLACK'S 32ND MOVE

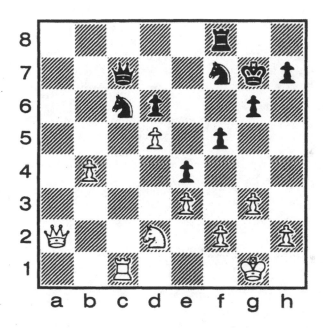

CLUE: White has one less piece than Black, but Black's Knight at c6 is pinned to its Queen by White's Rook at c1 and subject to capture next move. But what's pinned can be unpinned, as Fischer demonstrated.

SOLUTION: The salvation was 1 . . . Qa7!, breaking the pin with a gain of time. White loses his Queen if he captures the Knight. And if he tries 2. Qb2+, Black saves both the Knight and King with 2 . . . Nc-e5. Korchnoi elected to trade Queens but eventually resigned the futile ending on the 44th move. (0-1)

Manuel Aaron vs Bobby Fischer

STOCKHOLM, 1962
INTERZONAL TOURNAMENT
BLACK'S 29TH MOVE

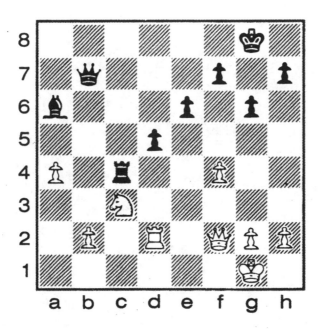

CLUE: White saw no access to his revered King. But Fischer delights in creating his own entree.

SOLUTION: Fischer's open-sesame was a simple capture 1 ... **Rxc3!**. If White takes back, he unlocks the b-file and Black checks 2 ... Qb1 +, leading to mate, the f1 square being attacked by Black's Bishop. White resigned. **(0-1)**

Bobby Fischer vs Ismet Ibrahimoglu

SIEGEN, 1970
19TH OLYMPIAD
WHITE'S 37TH MOVE

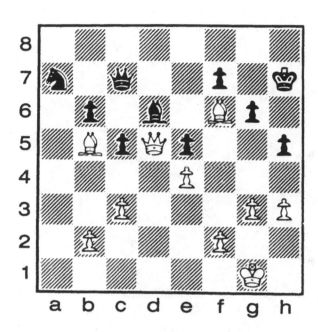

CLUE: White clearly has a spatial advantage, with two Bishops and a centralized Queen. Still, it's vague how to convert the intangible into the material.

SOLUTION: The powerful invasion **1. Be8!** immediately points out the strength of White's Bishop pair. Black had to answer **1 . . . Kg8**, defending the f-pawn, and White then exploited Black's overloaded pieces with **2. Bxf7 + Qxf7 3. Qxd6**. A pawn down, about to lose another, Black resigned. **(1-0)**

Bobby Fischer vs Eleazar Jimenez

HAVANA, 1966
17TH OLYMPIAD
WHITE'S 29TH MOVE

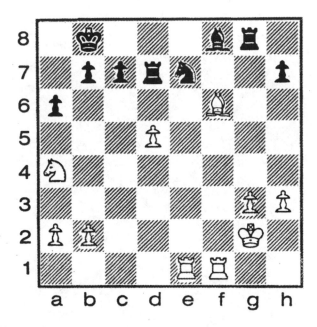

CLUE: White's 1. Nc5 move appears strong, but Black can play 1 . . . Rxd5. Make some room and you have Fischer's ploy.

SOLUTION: Eureka! The clearing sacrifice **1. d6!**, is just what the doctor ordered. After **1 . . . cxd6 2. Bxe7 Bxe7** (2 . . . Rxe7 loses to 3. Rxf8+ Rxf8 4. Rxe7) **3. Rf7**, Black resigned. Fischer must win material. If 3 . . . Re8, then 4. Nb6 Rc7 5. Nd5, taking advantage of the square made vacant by **1. d6!** (this push also drew away the protection for the square b6). **(1-0)**

Arinbjorn Gudmundsson vs Bobby Fischer

REYKJAVIK, ICELAND, 1960
BLACK'S 26TH MOVE

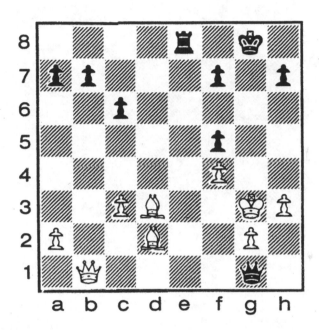

CLUE: White enjoys a slight material advantage (two Bishops against a Rook and pawn), but his King is highly susceptible to attack. Decision: Should Black exchange Queens or try to continue his offensive?

SOLUTION: The attack doesn't lead anywhere, whereas the Queen exchange 1 . . . Qxb1! 2. Bxb1 wins one of the two Bishops after 2 . . . **Re2!**. White resigned, for 3. Bc1 allows the skewer 3 . . . Re1. (0-1)

Bobby Fischer vs Klaus Darga

WEST BERLIN, 1960
EXHIBITION GAME
WHITE'S 27TH MOVE

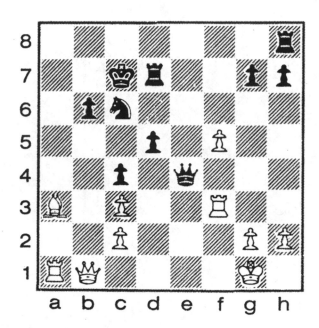

CLUE: White's warfare on the Queenside seems to have reached a standstill. With a Bishop powerfully posted at a3, what could be wrong?

SOLUTION: Nothing's wrong, but the Bishop posted at f4 would be more right. Fischer played **1. Bc1!** (he's not retreating, just advancing backward). The game continued: 1 . . . **Qe1+ 2. Rf1 Qxc3 3. Bf4+ Kb7 4. Qb5!**, threatening the heart-stopping 5. Qa6, a criss-cross mate (the controlled diagonals a6-c8 and b8-f4 cross). Black resigned, for neither 5 . . . Nb8 (6. Bxb8 threatening 7. Qxd7) nor 5 . . . Ra8 (6. Rxa8 Kxa8 7. Qxc6+) offers any real fight. **(1-0)**

Bobby Fischer vs Efim Geller

BLED, 1961
ALEKHINE MEMORIAL TOURNAMENT
WHITE'S 20TH MOVE

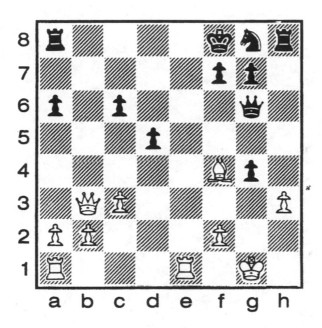

CLUE: This is a sharp position, with Black and White flailing away at each other's King. But it's White's turn, and he's ready for the execution.

SOLUTION: Fischer played the crunching **1. Qb7!**, directly threatening the Rook. Black can't answer 1 ... Re8 because of 2. Rxe8+ Kxe8 3. Re1+ winning Black's Queen or mating. The actual game went: **1 ... gxh3+** (a free pawn captured with discovered check) **2. Bg3 Rd8 3. Qb4+**, and Geller abdicated his King in light of 3 ... Ne7 4. Qxe7+ Kg8 5. Qxd8+. **(1-0)**

Bogdan Sliwa vs Bobby Fischer

WARSAW, 1962
USA VS POLAND MATCH
BLACK'S 34TH MOVE

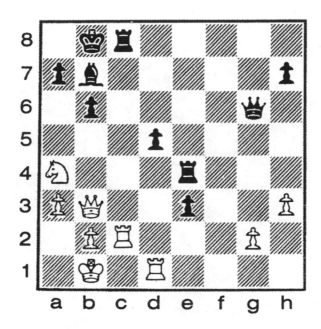

CLUE: White's pieces are prettily lined up along the a4-d1 diagonal—an ornamental, if inexorable, way to go.

SOLUTION: The lovely composition falls apart at the b1-g6 diagonal, which enables Fischer to win a piece by **1 . . . Rxc2!**. If White recaptures 2. Kxc2, Black discovers mate (2 . . . Rc4) thanks to the double check. And if White takes back 2. Qxc2, Black wins the Knight by 2 . . . Rxa4, when White's pinned Queen can't move off the b1-g6 line to capture Bobby's Rook. **(0-1)**

Georg Tringov vs Bobby Fischer

HAVANA—NEW YORK (BY TELETYPE), 1965
CAPABLANCA MEMORIAL TOURNAMENT
BLACK'S 20TH MOVE

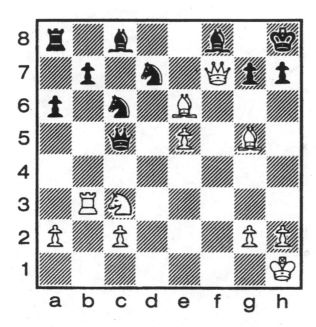

CLUE: White could mate next move at g8. Black's got to stop the mate and hold on to his extra material.

SOLUTION: Fischer consolidated the position with **1 . . . Nf6!**, guarding g8. Now 2. exf6 is met by 2 . . . Bxe6 3. Qxe6 (or 3. fxg7+ Bxg7 4. Qxe6, continuing as in the given variation) 3 . . . Qxg5, with Black keeping his additional piece and breaking White's attack. The game actually concluded: **2. Bxc8 Nxe5! 3. Qe6 Neg4!**, and White resigned in view of the threats to capture on c8 and to deliver mate by 4 . . . Nf2+ 5. Kg1 Nh3++ 6. Kh1 Qg1 mate. **(0-1)**

Bobby Fischer vs Paul Keres

CURACAO, 1962
CANDIDATES TOURNAMENT
WHITE'S 27TH MOVE

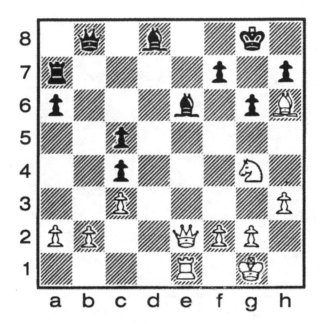

CLUE: White's pieces are the aggressors, though to no material gain yet. But Black is hard-pressed to defend weak pawns on the Queenside and weak squares on the Kingside, and his back row is shaky. Something's got to give.

SOLUTION: The crisp **1. Qxc4!** wins a pawn and Black can't take the Queen because of the mate along the back rank (1 . . . Bxc4 2. Re8 mate). Nor can Black go in for 1 . . . Qxb2 2. Rxe6! fxe6 3. Qxe6+, when 3 . . . Rf7 4. Qe8+ Rf8 5. Qxf8 is mate. Keres continued **1 . . . Qd6** and lost in 41 moves. **(1-0)**

Bobby Fischer vs Bent Larsen

PORTOROZ, YUGOSLAVIA, 1958
INTERZONAL TOURNAMENT
WHITE'S 22ND MOVE

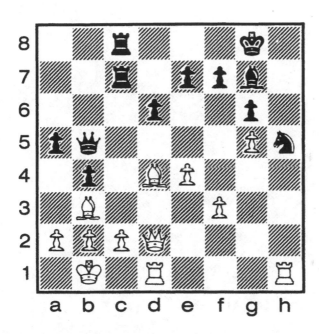

CLUE: White's Bishops, peering onto Black's Kingside, signal the end. Open the lines and mate.

SOLUTION: Fischer's final attack began with **1. Rxh5!**. After **1 . . . gxh5 2. g6** (sniping at the pinned f-pawn) **2 . . . e5 3. gxf7+ Kf8 4. Be3 d5 5. exd5** (5. Bxd5 weakens the c-pawn) **5 . . . Rxf7 6. d6** (attacking the Rook at f7) **6 . . . Rf6 7. Bg5 Qb7** (if 7 . . . Rg6, then 8. Be7+ Ke8 9. d7+ is crushing) **8. Bxf6 Bxf6 9. d7 Rd8 10. Qd6+**, Black resigned. If 10 . . . Be7, then 11. Qh6 is mate. And if 10 . . . Kg7, then 11. Rg1+ wins the Bishop at f6. **(1-0)**

Bobby Fischer vs Lhamsuren Miagmasuren

SOUSSE, TUNISIA, 1967
INTERZONAL TOURNAMENT
WHITE'S 29TH MOVE

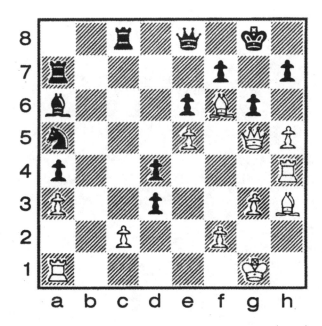

CLUE: White obviously has a powerful Kingside attack, but Black may be able to hold the position (1. Qh6, for example, is answered by 1 . . . Qf8, offering to trade Queens, dissipating White's assault). Fischer played a move so subtle that Black gave it little attention.

SOLUTION: Bobby repositioned his light-square Bishop by the devilishly obscure **1. Bg2!!.** Black should now have played 1 . . . Bb7, neutralizing White's King's Bishop, but he missed the point. Instead he continued 1 . . . **dxc2** and lost after **2. Qh6 Qf8 3. Qxh7 + !.** Black resigned, for 3 . . . Kxh7 4. hxg6 + + Kxg6 5. Be4 is mate. The point of **1. Bg2!!:** to be able to check from e4, mating Black in the above variation.
(1-0)

Bobby Fischer vs Svetozar Gligoric

BLED, 1959
CANDIDATES TOURNAMENT
WHITE'S 26TH MOVE

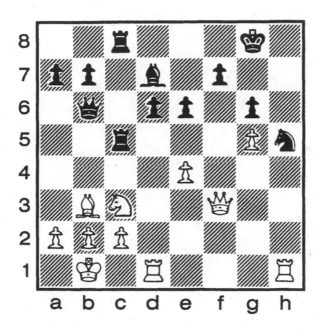

CLUE: Black seems to have his defenses in order, but a startling line-opener discombobulates any presumption of security.

SOLUTION: A familiar Fischer sacrifice **1. Rxh5!**, is the decisive breakthrough. In *My 60 Memorable Games,* Fischer says, "I've made this sacrifice so often, I feel like applying for a patent." The game continued: **1 . . . gxh5 2. Qxh5 Be8 3. Qh6!** (making sure the King can't run away) **3 . . . Rxc3** (hoping to create counterplay against White's King) **4. bxc3 Rxc3 5. g6!** (inflicting further weaknesses) **5 . . . fxg6 6. Rh1 Qd4 7. Qh7 +** and Black resigns (7 . . . Kf8 8. Rf1 + forces mate). **(1-0)**

Bobby Fischer vs Mark Taimanov

VANCOUVER, 1971
CANDIDATES MATCH 4TH GAME
WHITE'S 62ND MOVE

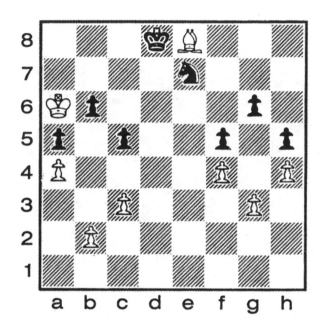

CLUE: If White moves his Bishop along the a4-e8 diagonal or plays it to f7, Black will have the time to defend his b-pawn. But why be mundane when you can rise to empyreal heights?

SOLUTION: Fischer boldly sacrificed his Bishop to get a mass of connected, dangerously advancing pawns **1. Bxg6!**. After 1 . . . **Nxg6 2. Kxb6 Kd7 3. Kxc5 Ne7 4. b4** (here they come!) **4 . . . axb4 5. cxb4 Nc8 6. a5 Nd6 7. b5 Ne4+ 8. Kb6 Kc8 9. Kc6 Kb8 10. b6**, Black resigned, for neither his King nor his Knight can contend with the parading pawns. **(1-0)**

Samuel Reshevsky vs Bobby Fischer

PALMA DE MALLORCA, 1970
INTERZONAL TOURNAMENT
BLACK'S 30TH MOVE

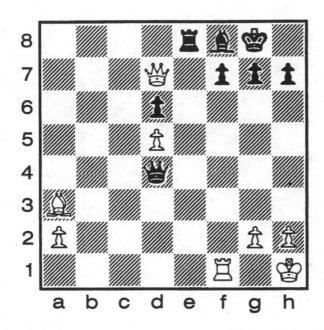

CLUE: White is intimidating Black's d-pawn, Rook, and King (particularly the f7 square). A single move by Black disposes of all three threats and compels White's resignation!

SOLUTION: Fischer dimmed White's hopes with **1 . . . Qf2!**, threatening 2 . . . Qxf1 mate. White gave up because 2. Rxf2 loses immediately to 2 . . . Re1 +, and there is no way to defend the Rook adequately. If 2. Qb5, for example, then 2 . . . Re1 wins. And if instead 2. Rg1, Black plays 2 . . . Re1 and the case is closed. **(0-1)**

Miguel Cuellar vs Bobby Fischer

SOUSSE, 1967
INTERZONAL TOURNAMENT
BLACK'S 30TH MOVE

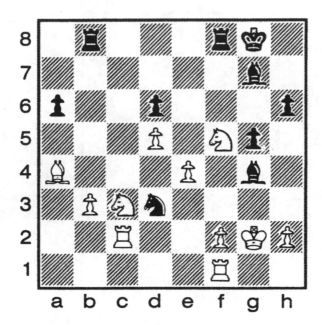

CLUE: White's got one more pawn than Black, but Fischer's got the attack and the neatest, simplest combination that anyone could imagine.

SOLUTION: The jump **1 . . . Nf4 + !** wins. If 2. Kh1, then 2 . . . Bf3 + 3. Kg1 Nh3 mate. If 2. Kg1 instead, then 2 . . . Bxf5 3. exf5 Bxc3, and White can't recapture because of 4 . . . Ne2 +, winning the Rook. The game therefore continued: **2. Kg3 Bxf5 3. exf5 Bxc3**, and as before, recapturing on c3 loses a Rook to Ne2 +. A piece ahead, Fischer had no trouble winning the ending. **(0-1)**

Edmar Mednis vs Bobby Fischer

NEW YORK, 1958-59
U.S. CHAMPIONSHIP
BLACK'S 37TH MOVE

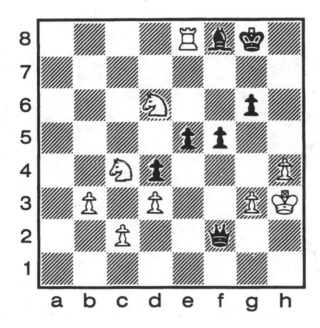

CLUE: In a materially imbalanced situation, Fischer relies on the single most powerful piece on the board.

SOLUTION: Fischer forced resignation with **1 . . . Qg1!**, threatening 2 . . . Qh1 mate. If White tries 2. g4, hoping to give his King breathing room, Black mates anyway with 2 . . . fxg4 mate. **(0-1)**

Ben Greenwald vs Bobby Fischer

POUGHKEEPSIE, 1963
NEW YORK STATE OPEN
BLACK'S 23RD MOVE

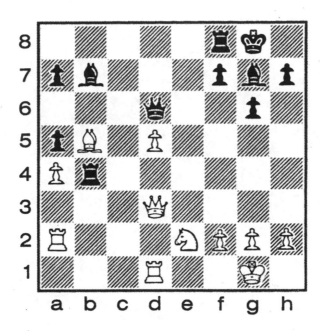

CLUE: It seems like an even game, with Fischer's two Bishops facing off against a Bishop and Knight. When nobody's going anywhere, it helps to get rid of wood.

SOLUTION: The reductive move was **1 . . . Qxd5!**. After White temporarily won a piece **2. Qxd5 Bxd5 3. Rxd5**, Black regained equality with **3 . . . Rb1+ 4. Nc1 Rxc1 + 5. Bf1 Re8** (threatening 6 . . . Re-e1) **6. f4 Re-e1 7. Rf2**. The final point was **7 . . . Bf8!**, for to cope with the impending 8 . . . Bc5, White would have had to surrender at least a Rook for a Bishop. **(0-1)**

Bobby Fischer vs Efim Geller

CURACAO, 1962
CANDIDATES TOURNAMENT
WHITE'S 43RD MOVE

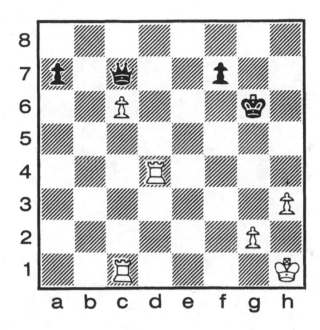

CLUE: Yet another chapter in the continuing saga of two Rooks versus a Queen. Here the Rooks are hungrier, supporting a mouth-watering c-pawn and leaning toward winning more material. How did Fischer consummate his play?

SOLUTION: The best move is **1. Ra4 !**, threatening the simple capture 2. Rxa7, when 2 . . . Qxa7 allows 3. c7 and 4. c8, making a new Queen. Nor does 1 . . . a5 save the pawn because of 2. Rxa5 anyhow. If Black then recaptures, White's c-pawn again Queens. Geller resigned. (1-0)

Jimmy Thomason vs Bobby Fischer

LINCOLN, NEBRASKA, 1955
U.S. JUNIOR CHAMPIONSHIP
BLACK'S 21ST MOVE

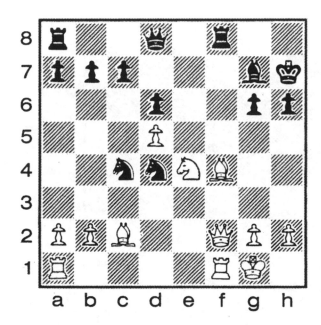

CLUE: White's f4-Bishop is pinned, but attacking it with the g-pawn runs into a discovered check (Nxg5). The answer's so simple even a twelve-year-old can see it.

SOLUTION: It helps if the twelve-year-old is Bobby Fischer. The direct **1 . . . Rxf4! 2. Qxf4 Ne2 + 3. Kh1 Nxf4** convinced White to resign. **(0-1)**

Raul Sanguinetti vs Bobby Fischer

PORTOROZ, 1958
INTERZONAL TOURNAMENT
BLACK'S 21ST MOVE

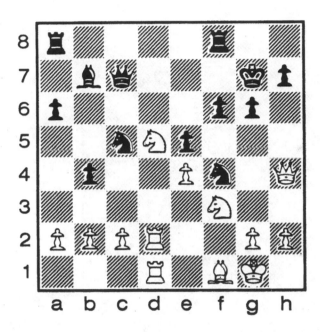

CLUE: It looks rather promising for White: doubled Rooks on the d-file, a menacing Knight at d5, and Kingside attacking chances. Too bad his Rooks have feet of clay.

SOLUTION: The direct **1 . . . Bxd5! 2. exd5 Ne4** plunders at least a Rook for a Knight, for the Rook at d2 can't move to a safe square. Fischer later converted this material gain into victory. **(0-1)**

Lajos Portisch vs Bobby Fischer

SANTA MONICA, CALIFORNIA, 1966
PIATIGORSKY CUP TOURNAMENT
BLACK'S 28TH MOVE

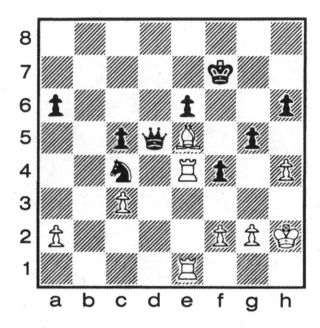

CLUE: Here comes another asymmetrical position: Fischer's Queen and Knight versus his opponent's two Rooks and Bishop. How does Bobby blitz the enemy forces?

SOLUTION: Fischer won the exchange (a Rook for a Knight) by **1 . . . Ne3!**. This cut the communication between the two Rooks. After **2. R1xe3 fxe3 3. Rxe3 Qxa2**, Fischer won in a few moves. **(0-1)**

Bobby Fischer vs Herman Pilnik

SANTIAGO, 1959
WHITE'S 33RD MOVE

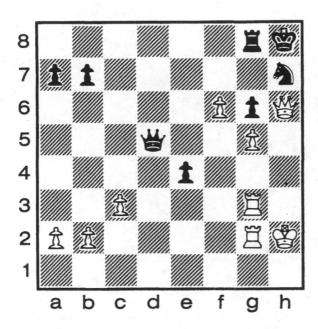

CLUE: Fischer could try to go about this steadfastly, but rather than deal with Black's defensive annoyances, he goes for broke.

SOLUTION: It's a blistering mate in two moves starting with **1. Qxh7 +!**. If 1 . . . Kxh7 then 2. Rh3 is mate. **(1-0)**

Ya'akov Bernstein vs Bobby Fischer

NETANYA, ISRAEL, 1968
BLACK'S 25TH MOVE

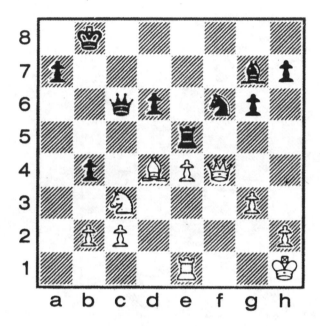

CLUE: A couple of pieces are hanging for both sides. The right move can save Black's and win White's.

SOLUTION: Fischer wins material with **1 . . . Rf5!**, when White's e-pawn is pinned to its King by Black's Queen and therefore can't capture the Rook at f5. White resigned, for after saving his attacked Queen, Black can safely capture White's Knight on c3. **(0-1)**

Izhak Aloni vs Bobby Fischer

VINKOVCI, YUGOSLAVIA, 1968
BLACK'S 44TH MOVE

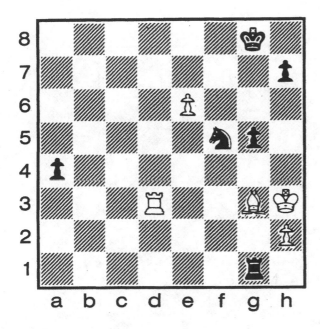

CLUE: White has a Bishop scrimmaging with a Knight and a far-advanced pawn. He also has his King off to the side of the board, about to fall off the edge.

SOLUTION: Black did White in with **1 . . . h5!**, threatening 2 . . . g4 mate. Against this there is no satisfactory defense. **(0-1)**

Boris Spassky vs Bobby Fischer

REYKJAVIK, 1972
WORLD CHESS CHAMPIONSHIP, 5TH MATCH GAME
BLACK'S 27TH MOVE

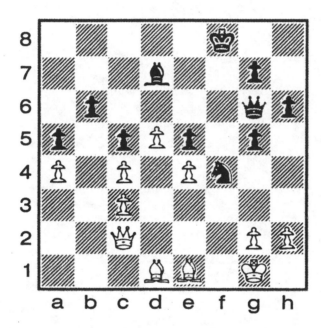

CLUE: They say Fischer played this move in a split second and that Spassky was jolted out of his seat!

SOLUTION: Spassky resigned after **1 . . . Bxa4!**, a punishing capture that can't be accepted. If 2. Qxa4, then 2 . . . Qxe4 threatens mate at both e1 and g2. After 2 . . . Qxe4 in this line, White could try 3. Kf2, but that loses to 3 . . . Nd3+ 4. Kg3 Qh4+ 5. Kf3 Qf4+ 6. Ke2 Nc1 mate! **(0-1)**

Bobby Fischer vs Oscar Panno

BUENOS AIRES, 1970
WHITE'S 28TH MOVE

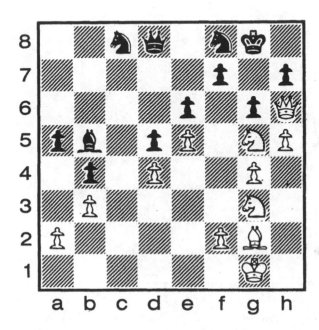

CLUE: White has an extremely aggressive position, but he still needs more ammo before this can be declared over.

SOLUTION: Fischer's remarkable salvo was **1. Be4!!**, transferring the Bishop immediately to a critical diagonal. At e4 the Bishop is immune from capture because 1 . . . dxe4 permits 2. N3xe4, menacing 3. Nf6 + and subsequent mate. Black tried the following defense: **1 . . . Qe7 2. Nxh7** (threatening 3. Nf6 +) **2 . . . Nxh7 3. hxg6 fxg6 4. Bxg6 Ng5 5. Nh5** (again threatening Nf6 +) **5 . . . Nf3 + 6. Kg2 Nh4 + 7. Kg3 Nxg6 8. Nf6 + !** (Black's Knight at g6 can't trot away) **8 . . . Kf7 9. Qh7 +** and mate next move (on 9 . . . Kf8 White mates by 10. Qg8). **(1-0)**

Robert Byrne vs Bobby Fischer

NEW YORK, 1963-64
U.S. CHAMPIONSHIP
BLACK'S 21ST MOVE

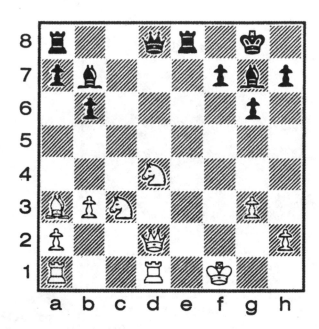

CLUE: What position could be more futile than this? Fischer is a piece behind and grandmasters in the analysis room are claiming he should resign. Outrageously, he didn't.

SOLUTION: Fischer played the incredibly quiet 1 . . . Qd7!, so quiet that top players were still saying Fischer should give it up. To his credit, it was Byrne who resigned instead! Just look: if White tries 2. Qf2, for example, then Fischer would have crowned the brilliancy with 2 . . . Qh3+ 3. Kg1 Re1+!! (deflecting the Rook at d1) 4. Rxe1 Bxd4, and Black is going to mate at g2 no matter how White plays. **(0-1)**

Bobby Fischer vs Reuben Shocron

MAR DEL PLATA, ARGENTINA, 1959
WHITE'S 40TH MOVE

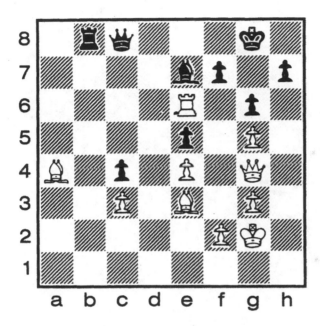

CLUE: Black's Queen pins White's Rook to its Queen, and the rook has no safe move—for now. Fischer concludes the game astonishingly.

SOLUTION: Fischer winds up a piece ahead after the stupefying **1. Bd7!**. If he doesn't take the Bishop and moves his Queen away, then White in turn can move his Rook to safety. And if Black takes at d7, then 2. Rxg6 + discovers an attack on Black's Queen. Shocron capitulated. **(1-0)**

Bobby Fischer vs Pal Benko

NEW YORK, 1965-66
U.S. CHAMPIONSHIP
WHITE'S 37TH MOVE

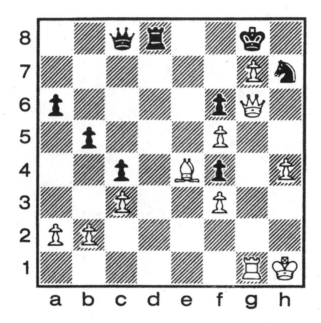

CLUE: White seems to be doing quite well, but how can he force an immediate outcome?

SOLUTION: By disrupting the defense. Benko resigned after the demolishing **1. Qe8 + !**. He realized that 1 . . . Rxe8 (moving off the d-file) allows 2. Bd5 +, after which Black would have to lose his Queen and Rook to temporarily halt the mating attack. **(1-0)**

Bobby Fischer vs Pal Benko

NEW YORK, 1963-64
U.S. CHAMPIONSHIP
WHITE'S 19TH MOVE

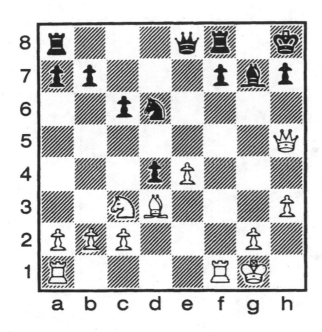

CLUE: White wants to play 1. e5, threatening 2. Qxh7 mate, but Black could defend on the brink with 1 . . . f5. Black must be so prevented.

SOLUTION: To dam up Black's f-pawn, Fischer gave away his Rook **1. Rf6!!**, an ingenious obstruction sacrifice. Black tried to flee with his King by **1 . . . Kg8** (seeing that 1 . . . Bxf6 loses to 2. e5 and 3. Qxh7 mate), but after **2. e5 h6 3. Ne2!** (taking the time-out to save his Knight) Black's position is as holey as Swiss cheese. If 3 . . . Nb5 (to counter 4. Rxd6), White wins with 4. Qf5, threatening mate at h7. And if 3 . . . Bxf6, then 4. Qxh6 leads to mate. Benko therefore resigned after 3. Ne2. **(1-0)**

Miguel Cuellar vs Bobby Fischer

STOCKHOLM, 1962
INTERZONAL TOURNAMENT
BLACK'S 36TH MOVE

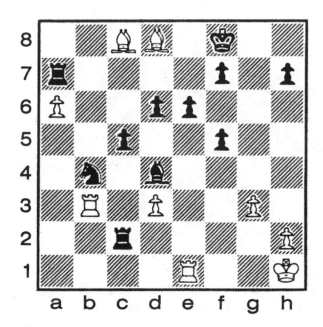

CLUE: If White had a couple of free moves and played Bb7 and Bb6, he'd trap Black's Rook at a7. He never got the chance.

SOLUTION: Fischer skewered the Bishops with **1 . . . Ra8!**, winning a piece. Inertia may explain White's playing another move **2. Bb6**, but he resigned after **2 . . . Rxc8**. (0-1)

Bobby Fischer vs Victor Ciocaltea

VARNA, 1962
15TH OLYMPIAD
WHITE'S 15TH MOVE

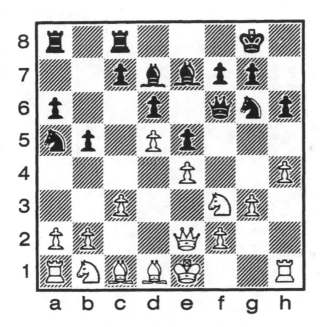

CLUE: It's late in the opening and nothing's been traded. In fact, the position is so log-jammed, it's hard to find any productive move, though not for Fischer.

SOLUTION: Bobby didn't miss that **1. Bg5!** actually traps the Queen. Even though Black can take the Bishop with his h-pawn 1 . . . hxg5, White's recapture 2. hxg5 gives an unanswerable pawn attack. Perhaps in shock, Ciocaltea played on a bit and then gave up. **(1-0)**

Laszlo Szabo vs Bobby Fischer

LEIPZIG, 1960
14TH OLYMPIAD
BLACK'S 21ST MOVE

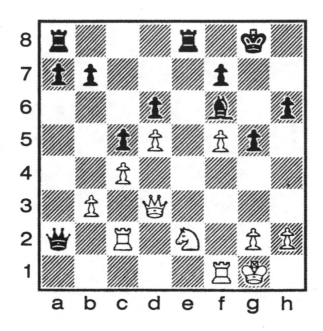

CLUE: Normally, an attack on a Queen from a Rook is sufficient to drive the stronger piece away. But Black here has an unimagined table-turner that leaves White helpless.

SOLUTION: The pulverizing intrusion **1 . . . Re3!** gives Fischer the upper hand. After **2. Qxe3** (2. Rxa2 Rxd3 saddles White with a difficult game) **2 . . . Qxc2 3. Kh1 a5 4. h4 a4**, Szabo resigned. As Fischer describes it, White's pawns now fall "like ripe apples." **(0-1)**

Wolfgang Unzicker vs Bobby Fischer

VARNA, 1962
15TH OLYMPIAD
BLACK'S 26TH MOVE

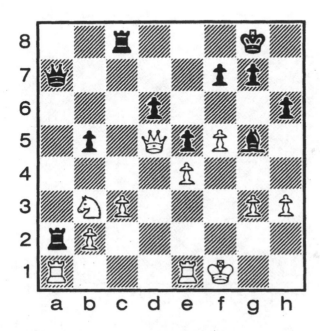

CLUE: White's King is exposed at f1, but still eludes attack. Black's Queen bears down along the a7-g1 diagonal and his Bishop is also strategically posted, but where's the support?

SOLUTION: From the Rooks: **1 . . . Rxc3!**, and if 2. bxc3, Black mates by 2 . . . Qf2, now that the 2nd rank has been ripped open. Meanwhile, 2. Rxa2 permits 2 . . . Rf3 +, with devastating consequences. For example, 3. Ke2 Rf2 + 4. Kd3 Qxa2, 5. Ra1 Qxb2 and White's future looks bleak; or 3. Kg2 Qf2 + 4. Kh1 Rxg3, with mate to follow. **(0-1)**

Bobby Fischer vs Mark Taimanov

VANCOUVER, 1971
CANDIDATES MATCH 2ND GAME
WHITE'S 85TH MOVE

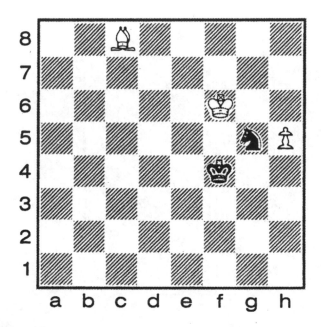

CLUE: Black hopes to sacrifice his Knight for White's pawn, leaving Fischer without enough mating force (a mere Bishop and King can't ever do it). The Knight could also give some pesky checks, if Fischer isn't careful.

SOLUTION: Fischer left Taimanov without a useful move with **1. Bf5!**, stopping potential checks at e4 and h7. Black went through the motions until his game stood still after **1 . . . Nf3** (the only plausible move he has) **2. h6 Ng5** (preparing to surrender the Knight if the pawn advances) **3. Kg6 Nf3** (again there is no other suitable move) **4. h7 Ne5 +** (4 . . . Nh4 + doesn't help stop the pawn either) **5. Kf6.** Finding no way to prevent the pawn from Queening, Black resigned. **(1-0)**

Bobby Fischer vs Byela Soos

SKOPJE, YUGOSLAVIA, 1967
WHITE'S 39TH MOVE

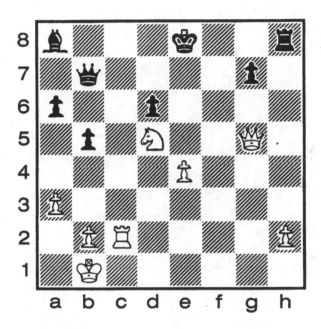

CLUE: White has several winning tries here, but only one of them forces instant mate.

SOLUTION: 1. Rc8 + !. If Black answers 1 . . . Qxc8, then 2. Qe7 is mate. Or if he plays 1 . . . Kd7 instead, then mate is 2. Qf5. And if the King runs in the other direction with 1 . . . Kf7, then 2. Qf5 still mates. **(1-0)**

Bobby Fischer vs Svetozar Gligoric

ROVINJ/ZAGREB, 1970
WHITE'S 35TH MOVE

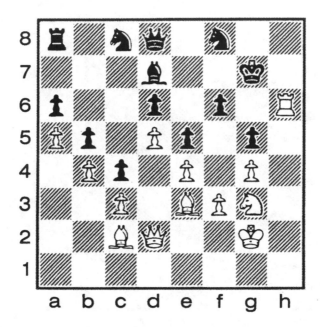

CLUE: White's Rook, in the heart of Black's camp, doesn't need to retreat just because it's attacked. This is the key to undermining the linchpin.

SOLUTION: Fischer played **1. Rxf6!**, and his opponent resigned. If Black captures the Rook with his King, 1 . . . Kxf6, then 2. Bxg5+ skewers the opposing Queen. And if he takes on f6 with his Queen 1 . . . Qxf6, then 2. Nh5+ forks the enemy King and Queen. Of course, if Black doesn't capture the Rook, it's apparent that 2. Bxg5 is crushing. **(1-0)**

Bobby Fischer vs Alberic O'Kelly

BUENOS AIRES, 1970
WHITE'S 35TH MOVE

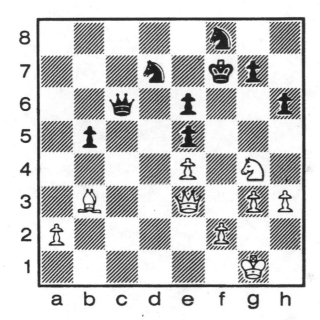

CLUE: Isolated doubled e-pawns can be strong (when they guard key central squares) or weak (when they fall victim to enemy piece attacks). Black seems to have everything defended until suddenly . . .

SOLUTION: White wins a pawn with **1. Nxe5 + ! Nxe5 2. Qf4 +**, forking Black's King and Knight at e5. **(1-0)**

Tigran Petrosian vs Bobby Fischer

BELGRADE, 1970
USSR VS THE REST-OF-THE-WORLD MATCH
BLACK'S 66TH MOVE

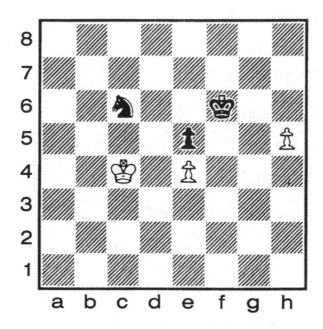

CLUE: Black can go for White's h-pawn with his King (1 . . . Kg5), but only at the cost of his e-pawn (2. Kd5, forcing the Knight to abandon its support). Sometimes the best offense is a solid defense.

SOLUTION: The send-off came with **1 . . . Nd4!**, anticipating 2. Kd5, which now is squashed by 2 . . . Nf3, defending the e-pawn from a secure haven. Fischer then collects the h-pawn with his King and heads back to team up with the Knight to win White's remaining pawn. **(0-1)**

Rene Letelier vs Bobby Fischer

LEIPZIG, 1960
14TH OLYMPIAD
BLACK'S 23RD MOVE

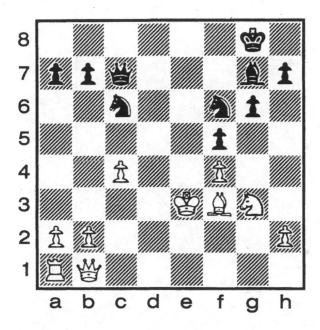

CLUE: White's King is airy but can get back to safety if given the time. That's not Fischer's way.

SOLUTION: The enemy King is immediately hounded by **1 . . . Qxf4 + !!**, an outrageously meteoric Queen sacrifice that can't be accepted (2. Kxf4) because of 2 . . . Bh6 mate. In the teeth of this furious onslaught (2. Kf2 Ng4 + 3. Kg2 Ne3 + 4. Kf2 Nd4), White resigned. **(0-1)**

Dr. Emil Nikolic vs Bobby Fischer

VINKOVCI, 1968
BLACK'S 31ST MOVE

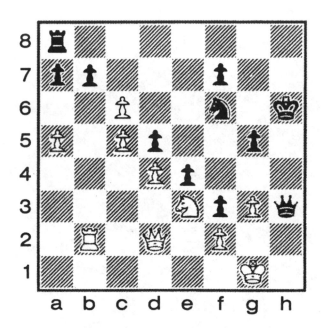

CLUE: Fischer mates at g2 with his Queen if White's Knight didn't command e3. He also mates at h1 if his Rook can occupy the h-file. And if he can guard h2 with another piece, his Queen mates by checking at h2 and then h1. One Black piece hinders these possibilities.

SOLUTION: The King! Thus **1 . . . Kg6!** actualizes all of Black's mating threats. One idea White now must stop—and can't—is 2 . . . Ng4, supporting the Queen's entry at h2, when 3. Nxg4 is prohibited because of 3 . . . Qg2 mate. Nikolic resigned. **(0-1)**

Bobby Fischer vs Dragojub Minic

VINKOVCI, 1968
WHITE'S 20TH MOVE

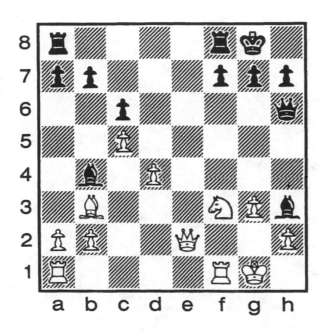

CLUE: White has latent pressure against the f7 square, but now his Rook at f1 is attacked by the Bishop at h3. Should he salvage the Rook?

SOLUTION: Sacrificing the Rook for the Bishop at h3 makes unarguable sense. A deadly massing of White's forces occurs after **1. Ne5!!**, allowing 1 . . . **Bxf1 2. Rxf1**, with a robust attack, especially against f7. Then Black tried **2 . . . Bd2** (to trade Queens by 3 . . . Qe3 +), but gave up after **3. Rf3 Ra-d8 4. Nxf7 Rxf7 5. Qe7!** (threatening 6. Qxf7 + as well as 6. Qxd8 +). **(1-0)**

Bobby Fischer vs Boris Spassky

REYKJAVIK, 1972
WORLD CHESS CHAMPIONSHIP MATCH 6TH GAME
WHITE'S 38TH MOVE

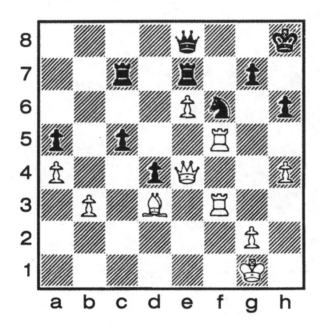

CLUE: Piece for piece, Fischer has a mobility advantage across the board. Black is also very weak on the light squares and White's e-pawn is a real menace to Black's community. The problem is getting through the clutter.

SOLUTION: Fischer elbowed through the maze with **1. Rxf6!**. After **1 . . . gxf6 2. Rxf6 Kg8 3. Bc4** (immobilizing the Rook at e7 because of the lurking discovery), **Kh8 4. Qf4**, Black resigned a hopeless position. **(1-0)**

Teodor Ghitescu vs Bobby Fischer

LEIPZIG, 1960
14TH OLYMPIAD
BLACK'S 14TH MOVE

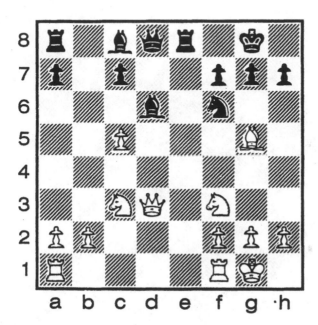

CLUE: White has just played an incredibly bad move, **1. d4xc5**, perhaps thinking it led to an exchange of Queens. Of course, blunders can lead to discoveries (as with Christopher Columbus and America).

SOLUTION: Instead of exchanging Queens, Black wins White's by **1 . . . Bxh2 + !** and 2 . . . Qxd3. A chagrined Ghitescu resigned. **(0-1)**

William Lombardy vs Bobby Fischer

NEW YORK, 1960-61
U.S. CHAMPIONSHIP
BLACK'S 30TH MOVE

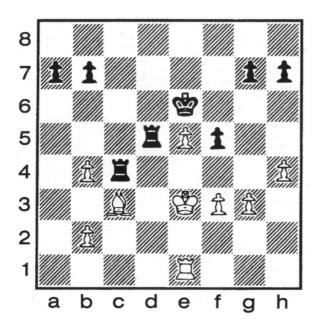

CLUE: Black is an exchange ahead (he has a Rook against a Bishop) but White has a protectable passed pawn. Not for long.

SOLUTION: Simplification is the key. After **1 . . . Rxc3 + !** (removing the e-pawn's guard) **2. bxc3 Rxe5 + 3. Kd2 Rxel 4. Kxel**, Fischer won the King-and-pawn ending. **(0-1)**

Bobby Fischer vs Moises Stekel

SANTIAGO, 1959
WHITE'S 35TH MOVE

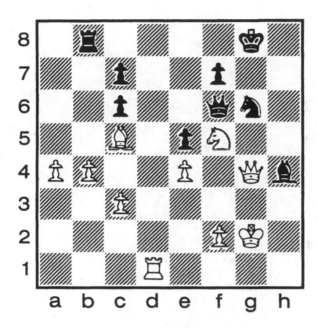

CLUE: Black flails away at defending a particular square, but it's all illusion.

SOLUTION: The telling move is **1. Be7!**, thieving a Bishop in broad daylight. Since Black's Knight is pinned and unable to guard e7, Black resigned. **(1-0)**

Bobby Fischer vs Jacek Bednarsky

HAVANA, 1966
17TH OLYMPIAD
WHITE'S 21ST MOVE

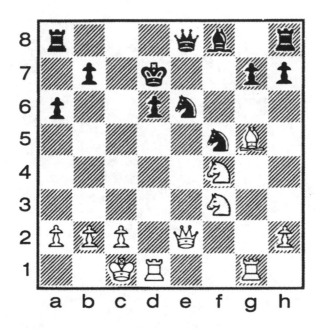

CLUE: Black's King is exposed and his pieces scattered. It's too much to hope that White doesn't have an outrageously crushing move.

SOLUTION: Like a bolt of lightning, the razing fork **1. Qe4!** attacks both Black's b-pawn and Knight at f5. After defending the Knight by **1 . . . g6**, Fischer expropriated his booty with **2. Nxe6.** Since if Qxe6 3. Qxb7 + , Black took note and resigned. **(1-0)**

Bent Larsen vs Bobby Fischer

DENVER, 1971
CANDIDATES MATCH 4TH GAME
BLACK'S 31ST MOVE

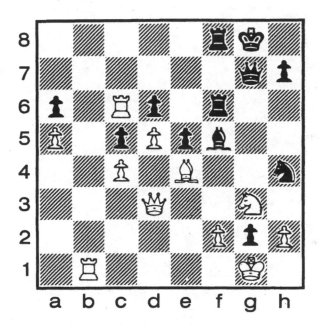

CLUE: They're fighting on two fronts, with White swarming the Queenside and Black storming the Kingside. Who's ahead doesn't matter, for an unexpected yet simple maneuver clinches matters.

SOLUTION: The elementary exchange **1 . . . Bxe4!** does the job. Since White's 2. Nxe4 loses his Queen after 2 . . . Nf3 + 3. Qxf3 Rxf3, he continued **2. Qxe4,** allowing **2 . . . Nf3 + 3. Kxg2 Nd2,** which forked Larsen's Queen and Rook. With White's f-pawn also threatened, it was time to surrender. **(0-1)**

Bobby Fischer vs Samuel Schweber

BUENOS AIRES, 1970
WHITE'S 23RD MOVE

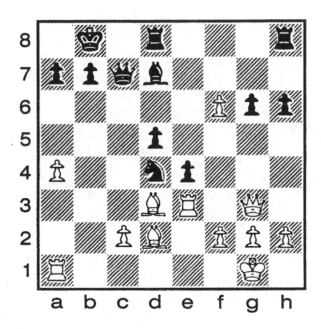

CLUE: This is a peculiar position. If White moves his attacked Bishop at d3, Black could opt to take the c-pawn with his Knight, forking the two Rooks. But White has a profound surprise in store for his wily opponent.

SOLUTION: Fischer struck with **1. Rxe4!!,** when 1 . . . dxe4 is answered by the pinning 2. Bf4. Even so, Black thought he could first exchange Queens and then take the Rook. But after 1 . . . **Qxg3,** Bobby blew his mind again with **2. Rxd4!!,** and Black's Queen amazingly has no exit! For example, if 2 . . . Qc7, then 3. Bf4 pins and regains the Queen. The game continued: **2 . . . Qg4 3. Rxg4 Bxg4 3. Bxg6,** and White's aggressive pieces and dangerous pawn soon led to recapturing the exchange. White won. **(1-0)**

Arthur Bisguier vs Bobby Fischer

NEW YORK, 1966-67
U.S. CHAMPIONSHIP
BLACK'S 69TH MOVE

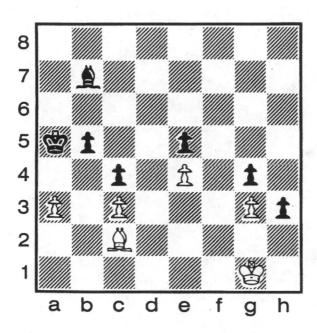

CLUE: White has everything secured, and Black's King is kept out of the game by White's Bishop at c2 guarding a4. An opaque situation that requires an explosive move to break things open.

SOLUTION: The deflecting sacrifice **1 . . . Bxe4!** lets through the light of day. After **2. Bxe4 Ka4 3. Bf5 Kb3 4. Bxg4 e4 5. Bxh3 Kxc3 6. g4 Kd2,** White resigned. There's no way White can stop both the e-pawn and the c-pawn from going in. Note that at d2, Fischer's King ideally guards the c1 and e1 promotion squares. **(0-1)**

Bobby Fischer vs Mr. Beach

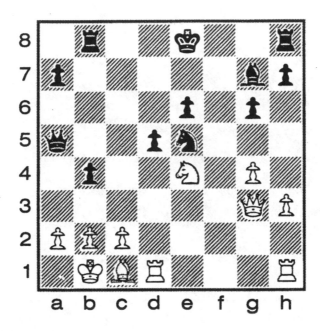

CLUE: The dark squares are the weak links in Black's chain, and the steadfast Bishop at g7 holds them together. How to knock it off is the name of the game.

SOLUTION: Fischer struck at the underpinnings with **1. Bh6!,** when 1 . . . Bxh6 is answered by 2. Qxe5, forking two Rooks and the e-pawn. Black tried to glue things together with 1 . . . **Qc7,** but a new bolt **2. Nd6 + !,** created fresh problems (if 2 . . . Qxd6, then 3. Bxg7 nails the Knight at e5 and the Rook at h8 simultaneously). Black recoiled his King out of check **2 . . . Kd8,** losing his Knight after **3. Bxg7 Qxg7 4. Qxe5!.** Black resigned, for 4 . . . Qxe5 is met with the forking 5. Nf7 + and 6. Nxe5, putting Fischer a piece ahead. **(1-0)**

Sven Johannessen vs Bobby Fischer

HAVANA, 1966
BLACK'S 26TH MOVE

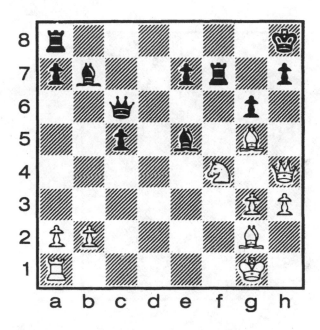

CLUE: White's attack has so far failed and he's an exchange down, but Fischer must defend accurately or White can still generate pesky counterplay. An incisive move is called for.

SOLUTION: Nothing's more pointed than **1 . . . Rxf4!**, reducing the position to bare bones. White resigned in view of 2. Bxc6 Rxh4 3. Bxb7 Rxh3 4. Bxa8 Rxg3+, and after the White King moves Black takes the Bishop at g5, leaving Fischer several pawns ahead; or 2. gxf4 (or 2. Bxf4) Qxg2 mate. **(0-1)**

Bobby Fischer vs Ludek Pachman

LEIPZIG, 1960
14TH OLYMPIAD
WHITE'S 38TH MOVE

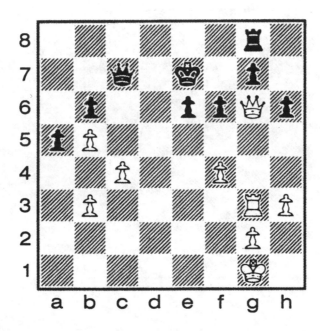

CLUE: It's a principle that if you're ahead in material, you should exchange pieces with a view to the endgame and eliminating counterplay. How banal, yet how sagacious in this case.

SOLUTION: Wholesale exchanges were initiated with **1. Qxg7 + !.** After 1 . . . **Rxg7 2. Rxg7 +** (skewering Queen and King) **2 . . . Kd6 3. Rxc7 Kxc7 4. g4,** Black soon abandoned the losing endplay. **(1-0)**

Bobby Fischer vs Olivio Gadia

MAR DEL PLATA, 1960
WHITE'S 23RD MOVE

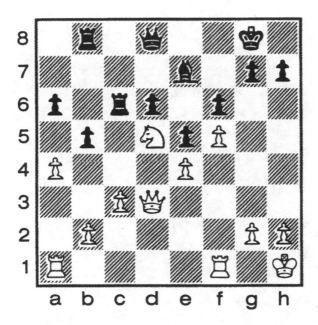

CLUE: Black's pieces are not coordinating well, and White's unassailable Knight sits powerfully in the center. Compare it to Black's Bishop, a blocked piece with no scope. Against these drawbacks, however, it's not the Knight that cemented White's superiority.

SOLUTION: Good Knight or not, Fischer readily ceded it **1. Nxe7 + !,** for if 1 . . . Qxe7, then 2. Qd5+ picks off the misplaced Rook. **(1-0)**

Bobby Fischer vs Miguel Najdorf

VARNA, 1962
15TH OLYMPIAD
WHITE'S 14TH MOVE

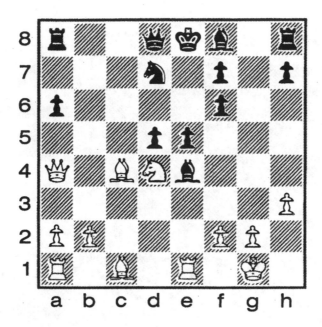

CLUE: Fischer's ready for business. His King is safely castled and he's better developed than Black, whose King may suddenly find itself stuck in the center. Quick, quick, before Black has a chance to complete his development and get his King to safety!

SOLUTION: Fischer demolished Black with the timely **1. Rxe4!.** The game continued: **1 . . . dxe4** (1 . . . dxc4 is answered by 2. Nf5, and Black doesn't even have material compensation for his troubles) **2. Nf5! Bc5** (else White plays 3. Qb3 with an irresistible attack against the f-pawn) **3. Ng7+** (so that Najdorf loses the right to castle) **3 . . . Ke7 4. Nf5+ Ke8 5. Be3,** and Fischer's powerful position was transmuted into a win after **5 . . . Bxe3 6. fxe3 Qb6** (to protect d6 from checks) **7. Rd1 Ra7 8. Rd6 Qd8 9. Qb3 Qc7 10. Bxf7+ Kd8 11. Be6.** A grandly conceived campaign! **(1-0)**

Bobby Fischer vs Mr. Bennet

SAN FRANCISCO, 1957
U.S. JUNIOR CHAMPIONSHIP
WHITE'S 38TH MOVE

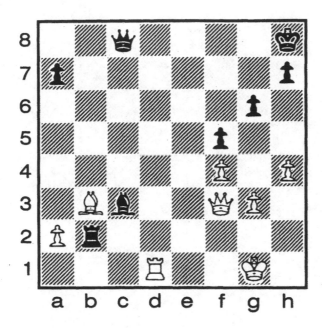

CLUE: Two open diagonals are involved: the light-squared b3-g8 and the dark-squared c3-h8. Your move, Bobby.

SOLUTION: Fischer dispatched his opponent with **1. Rd8 + !**, which wins the Queen or mates (as in the game) after **1 . . . Qxd8 2. Qxc3 +** (White's domination of both long diagonals is crushing) **2 . . . Qf6 3. Qxf6 mate. (1-0)**

Donald Byrne vs Bobby Fischer

NEW YORK, 1956
ROSENWALD TROPHY TOURNAMENT
BLACK'S 17TH MOVE

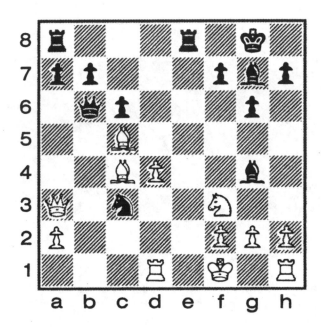

CLUE: Black's Queen and Knight are both under attack, and perhaps if he saves one he loses the other. These threats didn't deter the then thirteen-year-old Bobby Fischer from triumphing in what has been called the "Game of the Century."

SOLUTION: He played the out-of-this-world **1 . . . Be6!!.** The game continued: **2. Bxb6** (2. Bxe6 loses to 2 . . . Qb5+ 3. Kg1 Ne2+ 4. Kf1 Ng3++ 5. Kg1 Qf1+! 6. Rxf1 Ne2 mate) **2 . . . Bxc4+ 3. Kg1 Ne2 +** (to win the d-pawn with a gain of time, clearing the g7-a1 diagonal) **4. Kf1 Nxd4+ 5. Kg1 Ne2+ 6. Kf1 Nc3+ 7. Kg1 axb6,** and Fischer subsequently won in five-star fashion. Undoubtedly, the greatest combination ever germinated by a child prodigy. **(0-1)**

Bobby Fischer vs Mikhail Tal

BLED, 1961
WHITE'S 23RD MOVE

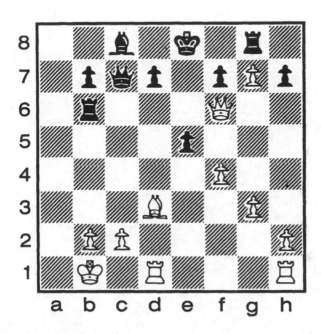

CLUE: Black has just uncovered an attack to White's Queen by the Rook at b6 (his pawn moved from e6 to e5). Fischer could swap down to an ending (1. Qxe5+ Qxe5 2. fxe5 Rxg7), but Tal, though a pawn down, would have some drawing chances. Time to pluck a rabbit out of a hat, or an outrageous move.

SOLUTION: Fischer divined the remarkable **1. fxe5!!**, appreciating that **1 . . . Rxf6 2. exf6** (with Bxh7 on the agenda) **2 . . . Qc5 3. Bxh7 Qg5** (trying to win White's expansive pawns) **4. Bxg8 Qxf6 5. Rh-f1 Qxg7 6. Bxf7+ Kd8 7. Be6** gives White a conquering hand. Bobby won in 47 moves. **(1-0)**

Bobby Fischer vs Dr. Reuben Fine

NEW YORK, 1963
SKITTLES GAME
WHITE'S 17TH MOVE

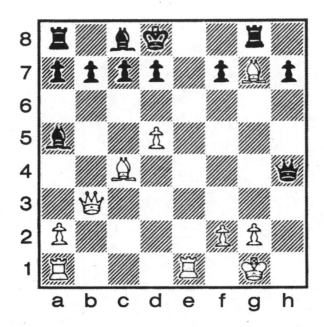

CLUE: The opening was an Evans Gambit (1. e4 e5 2. Nf3 Nc6 3. Bc4 Bc5 4. b4), one of the most exciting and romantic ways to start a game. The ending, though, was bluntly realistic.

SOLUTION: Fischer left Black tongue-tied and without a good move by **1. Qg3!** Dr. Fine resigned, unable to both save his Queen and stop mate. If 1 . . . Qxg3, then 2. Bf6 mate follows. Otherwise, White simply captures the hanging Queen. **(1-0)**

Bobby Fischer vs Mr. Finegold

BAY CITY, MICHIGAN, 1963
WESTERN OPEN
WHITE'S 49TH MOVE

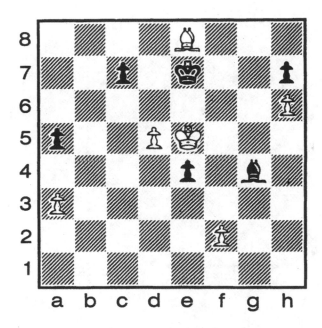

CLUE: White's Bishop, attacked, will be captured if it moves along the e8-h5 diagonal. Yet retreating on the a4-e8 diagonal may be too slow, giving Black time to defend. Never fear, the right move is already here.

SOLUTION: The shot heard round the board was **1. Bg6!**. Taking White's Bishop allows the h-pawn to Queen. Fischer won a couple of pawns and the game after **1 . . . Bd7 2. Bxh7 c5 3. dxc6 e.p. Bxc6 4. Bxe4 Bxe4 5. Kxe4 Kf6 6. f4.** (1-0)

Bobby Fischer vs Hans Ree

NETANYA, 1968
WHITE'S 17TH MOVE

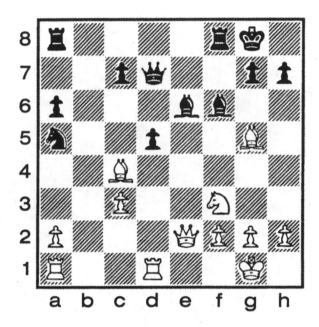

CLUE: Sure, Black is developed, but isn't he vulnerable along the a2-g8 diagonal? White jarringly wins a pawn.

SOLUTION: Fischer sacked his Queen **1. Qxe6 + !**, but after **1 . . . Qxe6,** won it back and gained a pawn with **2. Bxd5.** Black's Queen can't run away because it's pinned. Fischer won shortly thereafter. **(1-0)**

Arthur Bisguier vs Bobby Fischer

NEW YORK, 1960-61
U.S. CHAMPIONSHIP
BLACK'S 29TH MOVE

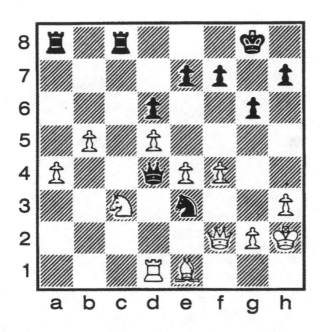

CLUE: White has approximate equality, with a Bishop and two connected (though attackable) passed pawns. He's menacing Fischer's Queen, and all White's pieces seem guarded. If 1 ... Nxd1, then Black loses his Queen to 2. Qxd4, but therein lies a combination to be unlocked.

SOLUTION: The key is 1 ... **Qxc3!**, swapping the Queen for Rook, Bishop, and Knight. Play continued: **2. Bxc3 Nxd1** (forking the Queen and Bishop) **3. Qd4 Nxc3**, and Black eventually won. (0-1)

Bobby Fischer vs Dr. Erwin Nievergelt

ZURICH, 1959
WHITE'S 17TH MOVE

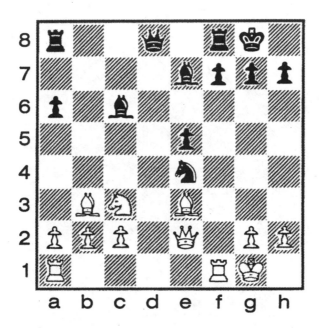

CLUE: There are a number of loose pieces and pawns in Black's position and it's simply a matter of determining the most advantageous way of devouring them.

SOLUTION: The Bishop at c6 is unguarded and vulnerable as **1. Rxf7! Rxf7 2. Bxf7+** shows. Black responded **2 . . . Kh8** (instead of taking the Bishop), for on 2 . . . Kxf7, White plays 3. Qc4+, also threatening the c6-Bishop. Fischer ended up a pawn ahead and subsequently won. **(1-0)**

Bobby Fischer vs Peter Dely

SKOPJE, 1967
WHITE'S 16TH MOVE

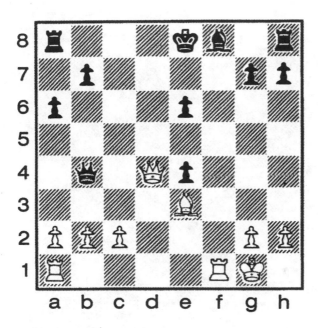

CLUE: Fischer's pieces are poised for the kill, and Black is just barely holding on, with his Queen, defended by the Bishop at f8, plugging the gap. Fischer's move changes everything.

SOLUTION: Black's game fell apart after **1. Rxf8 + !**, forcing **1 . . . Qxf8** in order to save the undefended Black Queen. Black gave up when he saw Fischer's **2. Qa4 +**. He can't play 2 . . . Ke7 because of 3. Bc5 +, skewering the Queen diagonally; nor can Black play 2 . . . Kf7 because of 3. Rf1 +, skewering the Queen vertically. On 2 . . . Kd8, White has a number of winning continuations, including 3. Bb6 + Kc8 4. Qc4 + with a penetrating attack. Finally, 2 . . . b5 is too weakening, as Black's position collapses after 3. Qxe4. **(1-0)**

Bobby Fischer vs Samuel Reshevsky

NEW YORK, 1958-59
U.S. CHAMPIONSHIP
WHITE'S 10TH MOVE

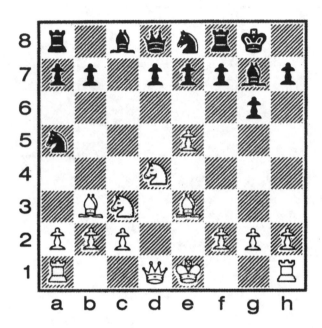

CLUE: Black is really cramped on the back rank and his Knight on a5 is out on a limb. Fischer's superior mobility and central concentration zooms doom.

SOLUTION: The winning sacrifice was **1. Bxf7 + !!.** In all lines Black loses his Queen for insufficient material: 1 . . . Rxf7 2. Ne6, and Black's Queen doesn't have a safe square, while the d-pawn is pinned by White's Queen; 1 . . . Kh8 2. Ne6 with the same result as before; and **1 . . . Kxf7** (which is what Reshevsky played) **2. Ne6!** (if 2 . . . Kxe6, then 3. Qd5 + Kf5 4. g4 + Kxg4 5. Rg1 + Kh4 6. Bg5 + Kh5 7. Qd1 + Rf3 8. Qxf3 mate) **2 . . . dxe6 3. Qxd8** and Fischer won the ending. **(1-0)**

Jose Agdamus vs Bobby Fischer

BUENOS AIRES, 1970
BLACK'S 35TH MOVE

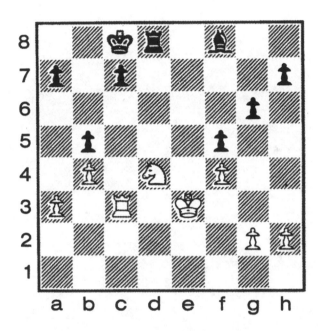

CLUE: Fischer has a pawn more than his opponent, but White's pieces could counterthreat if given the chance. There's an almost simplistic method to stop them.

SOLUTION: Black could have exchanged pieces by 1 . . . Bg7 2. Rd3 Bxd4+ 3. Rxd4 Rxd4 4. Kxd4, but White's King is too well centralized. The surest way is **1 . . . Rxd4! 2. Kxd4 Bg7+**. Though all the pieces get traded off, White's King ends up one square back on c3, and Bobby wins. **(0-1)**

A Collection of 101 Fischer Games in Algebraic Notation

The following are the complete game scores in algebraic notation for *Bobby Fischer's Outrageous Chess Moves* presented in this book. They should provide great pleasure and instructional value.

GAME 1

1. e4	c5	17. Re1	Qxe4	33. Bc3	Rdxc4
2. Nf3	d6	18. Rxe4	d5	34. Bxc4	Rxc4
3. d4	cxd4	19. Rg3	g6	35. Kd3	Rc5
4. Nxd4	Nf6	20. Bxd5	Bd6	36. Rxa5	Rxa5
5. Nc3	Nc6	21. Rxe6	Bxg3	37. Bxa5	Bxb2
6. Bc4	e6	22. Re7	Bd6	38. a4	Kf8
7. Bb3	Be7	23. Rxb7	Rac8	39. Bc3	Bxc3
8. Be3	O-O	24. c4	a5	40. Kxc3	Ke7
9. O-O	Bd7	25. Ra7	Bc7	41. Kd4	Kd6
10. f4	Qc8	26. g3	Rfe8	42. a5	f6
11. f5	Nxd4	27. Kf1	Re7	43. a6	Kc6
12. Bxd4	exf5	28. Bf6	Re3	44. a7	Kb7
13. Qd3	fxe4	29. Bc3	h5	45. Kd5	h4
14. Nxe4	Nxe4	30. Ra6	Be5	46. Ke6	(1–0)
15. Qxe4	Be6	31. Bd2	Rd3		
16. Rf3	Qc6	32. Ke2	Rd4		

GAME 2

1. e4	c6	13. c4	Rad8	25. Rxd5	f5
2. Nc3	d5	14. Bc2	Bxc2	26. Ne5+	Bxe5
3. Nf3	dxe4	15. Kxc2	f5	27. Rxe5	Nf6
4. Nxe4	Nf6	16. Rhe1	f4	28. Rxe8	Nxe8
5. Nxf6+	exf6	17. Bd2	Nf6	29. Be5	Kh5
6. Bc4	Bd6	18. Ne5	g5	30. Kd3	g4
7. Qe2+	Qe7	19. f3	Nh5	31. b4	a6
8. Qxe7+	Kxe7	20. Ng4	Kg7	32. a4	gxf3
9. d4	Bf5	21. Bc3	Kg6	33. gxf3	Kh4
10. Bb3	Re8	22. Rxe8	Rxe8	34. b5	axb5
11. Be3	Kf8	23. c5	Bb8	35. a5	Kh3
12. O-O-O	Nd7	24. d5	cxd5	36. c6	(1–0)

GAME 3

1. e4	e5	19. Bc2	Bd7	37. Qxg4	Qe6
2. Nf3	Nc6	20. Bh6	Rfe8	38. Qxe6	Rxe6
3. Bb5	a6	21. h4	Bg7	39. Red1	Rd8
4. Ba4	Nf6	22. Bg5	f6	40. a4	bxa4
5. O-O	Be7	23. Bc1	Bf8	41. Rxa4	Nb7
6. Re1	b5	24. h5	g5	42. Rd5	Rc6
7. Bb3	d6	25. Qg3	Qg7	43. c4	Kg8
8. c3	O-O	26. Nh2	h6	44. c5	Kf7
9. h3	Nd7	27. Ng4	Qf7	45. Rb4	Rb8
10. d4	Nb6	28. Qf3	Bg7	46. Rd7+	Ke6
11. dxe5	Nxe5	29. Ne3	Be6	47. Rh7	Rb6
12. Nxe5	dxe5	30. Nf5	Bf8	48. cxb6	Bxb4
13. Qh5	Bf6	31. b3	Rad8	49. bxc7	Rc8
14. Nd2	g6	32. Be3	Rd7	50. Nf5	Bf8
15. Qf3	Qe7	33. Qh3	Kh7	51. g4	Na5
16. Qg3	Bh4	34. Bd1	Nc8	52. b4	Bxb4
17. Qh2	Bf6	35. Bg4	Nd6	53. Bd2	(1-0)
18. Nf3	Be6	36. Ng3	Bxg4		

GAME 4

1. e4	e6	15. Qh4	Nd5	29. g4	Ke8
2. d3	c5	16. Qxd8	Rxd8	30. Rf1	Rd5
3. Nf3	Nc6	17. a4	Rad7	31. Rf3	Rd8
4. g3	g6	18. Bf1	Bxf1	32. Rh3	Bf8
5. Bg2	Bg7	19. Kxf1	Nde7	33. Nxa5	Rc7
6. O-O	Nge7	20. Nc4	Nc8	34. Nc4	Ra7
7. c3	O-O	21. Bg5	N6e7	35. Nxb6	Nxb6
8. d4	d6	22. Nfd2	h6	36. Rxb6	Rda8
9. dxc5	dxc5	23. Bxe7	Rxe7	37. Nf6+	Kd8
10. Qe2	b6	24. Ra3	Rc7	38. Rc6	Rc7
11. e5	a5	25. Rb3	Rc6	39. Rd3+	Kc8
12. Re1	Ba6	26. Ne4	Bf8	40. Rxc7+	Kxc7
13. Qe4	Ra7	27. Ke2	Be7	41. Rd7+	Kc6
14. Nbd2	Bd3	28. f4	Kf8	42. Rxf7	(1-0)

GAME 5

1. e4	c6	13. Bxe7	Qxe7	25. Rhe1	Rxc6
2. d4	d5	14. Kb1	Rd8	26. Re5	Ra8
3. Nc3	dxe4	15. Qe4	b5	27. Be4	Rd6
4. Nxe4	Nd7	16. Bd3	a5	28. Bxa8	Rxd1+
5. Nf3	Ngf6	17. c3	Qd6	29. Kc2	Rf1
6. Nxf6+	Nxf6	18. g3	b4	30. Rxa5	Rxf2+
7. Bc4	Bf5	19. c4	Nf6	31. Kb3	Rh2
8. Qe2	e6	20. Qe5	c5	32. c5	Kd8
9. Bg5	Bg4	21. Qg5	h6	33. Rb5	Rxh3
10. O-O-O	Be7	22. Qxc5	Qxc5	34. Rb8+	Kc7
11. h3	Bxf3	23. dxc5	Ke7	35. Rb7+	Kc6
12. Qxf3	Nd5	24. c6	Rd6	36. Kc4	(1-0)

GAME 6

1. e4	c5	19. Re1 +	Kf8	37. Ka3	Qc2		
2. Nf3	d6	20. c3	h5	38. Nd3 +	Kf6		
3. d4	cxd4	21. f5	Rh6	39. Nc5	Qc1		
4. Nxd4	Nf6	22. f6	gxf6	40. Rxa4	Qe3		
5. Nc3	a6	23. Nf4	h4	41. Nxa6	f4		
6. Bg5	e6	24. Rd8 +	Kg7	42. Rd4	Kf5		
7. f4	Be7	25. Ree8	Qg1 +	43. Nb4	Qe7		
8. Qf3	Qc7	26. Kd2	Qf2 +	44. Kb3	Qxh4		
9. O-O-O	Nbd7	27. Ne2	Rg6	45. Nd3	g5		
10. Be2	b5	28. g3	f5	46. c4	Qg3		
11. Bxf6	Nxf6	29. Rg8 +	Kf6	47. c5	f3		
12. e5	Bb7	30. Rxg6 +	fxg6	48. Kc4	f2		
13. exf6	Bxf3	31. gxh4	Qxh2	49. Nxf2	Qxf2		
14. Bxf3	Bxf6	32. Rd4	Qh1	50. c6	Qxb2		
15. Bxa8	d5	33. Kc2	Ke5	51. Kc5	Qc3 +		
16. Bxd5	Bxd4	34. a4	Qf1	52. Kd5	g4		
17. Rxd4	exd5	35. Nc1	Qg2 +	53. Rc4	Qe5 mate		
18. Nxd5	Qc5	36. Kb3	bxa4 +	(0–1)			

GAME 7

1. e4	e5	11. d3	Bxh3	21. f4	Nd4
2. Nf3	Nc6	12. gxh3	Qd7	22. Qc4	Qg6
3. Bc4	Nf6	13. Bf3	Qxh3	23. c3	Nf5
4. Ng5	d5	14. Nd2	Rad8	24. fxe5	Rxe5
5. exd5	Na5	15. Bg2	Qf5	25. Bf4	Re2
6. Bb5 +	c6	16. Qe1	Rfe8	26. Be4	Rxb2
7. dxc6	bxc6	17. Ne4	Bb6	27. Be5	Re8
8. Be2	h6	18. Nxf6 +	Qxf6	28. Rxf5	Rxe5
9. Nh3	Bc5	19. Kh1	c5	29. Rxe5	(1–0)
10. O-O	O-O	20. Qc3	Nc6		

GAME 8

1. e4	e5	16. Qc2	Ne7	31. Bc4	Kf7
2. Nf3	Nc6	17. Ba3	Ng6	32. Bxe6 +	Kxe6
3. Bc4	Bc5	18. Rfd1	Nf4	33. Re1 +	Kf7
4. b4	Bxb4	19. Bf1	Kg8	34. Qc4 +	Kg6
5. c3	Ba5	20. Ne5	Qc7	35. Re7	Rhg8
6. d4	exd4	21. Nc4	Be6	36. Rae1	h5
7. O-O	d6	22. Nxd6	Rd8	37. Qf7 +	Kh6
8. Qb3	Qd7	23. e5	f6	38. R1e6	Rdf8
9. cxd4	Bb6	24. Bxc5	Bxc5	39. Rxf6 +	gxf6
10. Bb5	Kf8	25. Nce4	Bxd6	40. Qh7 +	Kg5
11. d5	Na5	26. exd6	Qc8	41. h4 +	Kg4
12. Qa4	c6	27. Nc5	Bd5	42. Re4 +	Kh3
13. dxc6	bxc6	28. d7	Qc7	43. Qf5 +	Rg4
14. Bd3	Nb7	29. g3	Ne6	44. Rxg4	hxg4
15. Nc3	Nc5	30. Nxe6	Bxe6	45. Qd3	(1–0)

GAME 9

1. b3	d5	16. Rg3	Bxe5	31. dxe4	c4
2. Bb2	c5	17. fxe5	f5	32. b4	Bg4
3. Nf3	Nc6	18. exf6	Rxf6	33. Ke3	Rd7
4. e3	Nf6	19. Qxg7+	Qxg7	34. g6+	Kf8
5. Bb5	Bd7	20. Rxf6	Qxg3	35. gxh7	Rxh7
6. O-O	e6	21. hxg3	Re8	36. Ng6+	Ke8
7. d3	Be7	22. g4	a4	37. Nxe5	Bc8
8. Bxc6	Bxc6	23. Nf3	axb3	38. Nxc4	Kd8
9. Ne5	Rc8	24. axb3	Kg7	39. Nd6	Rg7
10. Nd2	O-O	25. g5	e5	40. Kf2	Kc7
11. f4	Nd7	26. Nh4	Bd7	41. Nxc8	Kxc8
12. Qg4	Nxe5	27. Rd6	Be6	42. Rd6	(1–0)
13. Bxe5	Bf6	28. Kf2	Kf7		
14. Rf3	Qe7	29. Rb6	Re7		
15. Raf1	a5	30. e4	dxe4		

GAME 10

1. d4	Nf6	11. Nxd2	e5	21. exd4	Qe4
2. Nf3	g6	12. Nb3	O-O	22. Qg4	Qc2
3. Bf4	Bg7	13. Qc5	Rc8	23. g3	Qxa2
4. Nbd2	c5	14. Qb4	Re8	24. Bb5	Qd5
5. c3	cxd4	15. Be2	exd4	25. Bxe8	Qxh1+
6. cxd4	d5	16. Nxd4	Qh4	26. Ke2.	Rxe8+
7. Bxb8	Rxb8	17. Qxb7	Bxd4	27. Kd3	Be1
8. Qa4+	Bd7	18. Qxd7	Bxb2		(0–1)
9. Qxa7	Ne4	19. Rd1	Bc3+		
10. e3	Nxd2	20. Kf1	d4		

GAME 11

1. e4	e6	12. Nb5	Qb6	23. Bf2	Rfc8
2. d4	d5	13. O-O-O	Bd7	24. Bd3	Na2+
3. Nc3	Nf6	14. Nd6	Na4	25. Kd1	Nc3+
4. e5	Nfd7	15. Bb5	Nd4	26. Kc1	Rc5
5. f4	c5	16. Be3	Ne2+	27. Qh4	Ra5
6. dxc	Bxc5	17. Bxe2	Qxb2+	28. Kd2	h6
7. Qg4	O-O	18. Kd2	Qb4+	29. g4	fxg4
8. Bd3	f5	19. Kc1	Nc3	30. Rxg4	Kh8
9. Qh3	Bxg1	20. Rde1	Nxa2+	31. Qxh6+	(1–0)
10. Rxg1	Nc5	21. Kd1	Nc3+		
11. Bd2	Nc6	22. Kc1	d4		

GAME 12

1. d4	Nf6	18. a5	f6	35. Nd1	Ke6
2. Nf3	c5	19. axb6	axb6	36. Qxa2	Rxa2
3. c3	g6	20. Nd3	e5	37. Rb2	Ra1
4. g3	b6	21. Nf2	e4	38. Be1	Kd7
5. Bg2	Bb7	22. f4	Ra8	39. Bd2	Kc6
6. O-O	Bg7	23. Bd2	Rxa1	40. Be1	Na3
7. Nbd2	O-O	24. Qxa1	Ra8	41. Kd2	Kb5
8. Re1	d5	25. Qb1	Qc6	42. Bf2	Ka4
9. Ne5	Nc6	26. b3	Ba6	43. Be1	Be7
10. Ndf3	Rc8	27. Qb2	Bxf1	44. Bf2	Nb5
11. Nxc6	Bxc6	28. Rxf1	c4	45. Kc2	Ka3
12. Bh3	Bd7	29. b4	Qa4	46. Rb1	Ra2 +
13. Bf1	Bc6	30. Rb1	Bf8	47. Rb2	Nxc3
14. Ne5	Bb7	31. Kf1 —	Nb5	48. Kxc3	Ra1
15. a4	Ne4	32. Ke2	f5	(0–1)	
16. f3	Nd6	33. Nd1	Kf7		
17. e3	Qc7	34. Nf2	Qa2		

GAME 13

1. e4	e6	15. Bxd7	Bxf3	29. Qh8	Re7
2. d4	d5	16. gxf3	Qxd7	30. h6	Kf7
3. Nc3	Nf6	17. Rdg1	f6	31. Qh7 +	Kf8
4. Bg5	dxe4	18. Rxg7	Qxg7	32. Qd3	Kf7
5. Nxe4	Nbd7	19. Rxg7	Kxg7	33. h7	Rh5
6. Nf3	Be7	20. Qf4	Rac8	34. Qd5 +	Re6
7. Nxf6 +	Bxf6	21. h5	c5	35. f4	f5
8. h4	h6	22. Qg4 +	Kf7	36. fxe5	Rxh7
9. Bxf6	Qxf6	23. Qg6 +	Ke7	37. Qd7 +	Re7
10. Qd2	O-O	24. dxc5	Rxc5	38. Qxf5 +	Ke8
11. O-O-O	b6	25. Qxh6	Rg5	39. f4	Kd8
12. Bb5	Qe7	26. b3	e5	40. e6	(1–0)
13. Rh3	Bb7	27. Kb2	Rf7		
14. Rg3	Kh8	28. a4	Ke6		

GAME 14

1. e4	c5	14. f3	Rc8	27. Qf3	Qe6
2. Nf3	d6	15. Kb1	Nd7	28. Rc7	Rde8
3. d4	cxd4	16. h4	b5	29. Nf4	Qe5
4. Nxd4	Nf6	17. Bh3	Bxh3	30. Rd5	Qh8
5. Nc3	a6	18. Rxh3	Nb6	31. a3	h6
6. h3	Nc6	19. Bxb6	Qxb6	32. gxh6	Qxh6
7. g4	Nxd4	20. Nd5	Qd8	33. h5	Bg5
8. Qxd4	e5	21. f4	exf4	34. hxg6	fxg6
9. Qd3	Be7	22. Qxf4	Qd7	35. Qb3	Rxf4
10. g5	Nd7	23. Qf5	Rcd8	36. Re5 +	Kf8
11. Be3	Nc5	24. Ra3	Qa7	37. Rxe8 +	(1–0)
12. Qd2	Be6	25. Rc3	g6		
13. O-O-O	O-O	26. Qg4	Qd7		

GAME 15

1.	e4	c5
2.	Nf3	Nf6
3.	Nc3	d5
4.	Bb5+	Bd7
5.	e5	d4
6.	exf6	dxc3
7.	fxg7	cxd2+
8.	Qxd2	Bxg7
9.	Bd3	Qc7
10.	O-O	c4
11.	Be4	Nc6
12.	Qe2	c3
13.	bxc3	Bxc3
14.	Rb1	O-O-O
15.	Qc4	f5
16.	Qxc3	fxe4
17.	Ng5	Rhg8
18.	Nxe4	Nd4
19.	Qxc7+	Kxc7
20.	Ng3	Bc6
21.	Re1	Nxc2
22.	Rxe7+	Rd7
23.	Bf4+	Kc8
24.	Rxd7	Kxd7
25.	Rd1+	Kc8
26.	Nf5	Rxg2+
27.	Kf1	b6
28.	Ne7+	Kb7
29.	Nxc6	Rg4
	(1–0)	

GAME 16

1.	e4	e6
2.	d4	d5
3.	Nc3	Nf6
4.	Bg5	dxe4
5.	Nxe4	Be7
6.	Bxf6	Bxf6
7.	Nf3	Nd7
8.	Qd2	Be7
9.	O-O-O	Nf6
10.	Bd3	O-O
11.	Nxf6+	Bxf6
12.	Qf4	c5
13.	dxc5	Qa5
14.	Qc4	Be7
15.	h4	Qxc5
16.	Qe4	f5
17.	Qe2	b5
18.	Ng5	Bf6
19.	Nxe6	Bxe6
20.	Qxe6+	Kh8
21.	Kb1	Qxf2
22.	Qxf5	Qxf5
23.	Bxf5	g6
24.	Bd3	Rad8
25.	h5	Kg7
26.	hxg6	hxg6
27.	Bxb5	Rxd1+
28.	Rxd1	Rb8
29.	a4	a6
30.	Rd7+	Kh6
31.	Rd6	Bxb2
32.	Kxb2	axb5
33.	a5	Ra8
34.	a6	Kh5
35.	Kb3	g5
36.	Kb4	Kg4
37.	Kxb5	Kg3
38.	Rd7	g4
39.	a7	(1–0)

GAME 17

1.	e4	d5
2.	exd5	Qxd5
3.	Nc3	Qd8
4.	d4	Nf6
5.	Bc4	Bf5
6.	Qf3	Qc8
7.	Bg5	Bxc2
8.	Rc1	Bg6
9.	Nge2	Nbd7
10.	O-O	e6
11.	Bxf6	gxf6
12.	d5	e5
13.	Bb5	Be7
14.	Ng3	a6
15.	Bd3	Qd8
16.	h4	h5
17.	Bf5	Nb6
18.	Nce4	Nxd5
19.	Rfd1	c6
20.	Nc3	Qb6
21.	Rxd5	cxd5
22.	Nxd5	Qxb2
23.	Rb1	Qxa2
24.	Rxb7	(1–0)

GAME 18

1.	e4	c6
2.	d4	d5
3.	exd5	cxd5
4.	c4	Nf6
5.	Nc3	Nc6
6.	Nf3	Bg4
7.	cxd5	Nxd5
8.	Qb3	Bxf3
9.	gxf3	e6
10.	Qxb7	Nxd4
11.	Bb5+	Nxb5
12.	Qc6+	Ke7
13.	Qxb5	Nxc3
14.	bxc3	Qd7
15.	Rb1	Rd8

16. Be3	Qxb5	**23.** a4	Bg7	**30.** Bb8	Rc8
17. Rxb5	Rd7	**24.** Rb6 +	Kd5	**31.** a6	Rxc3
18. Ke2	f6	**25.** Rb7	Bf8	**32.** Rb5 +	Kc4
19. Rd1	Rxd1	**26.** Rb8	Bg7	**33.** Rb7	Bd4
20. Kxd1	Kd7	**27.** Rb5 +	Kc6	**34.** Rc7 +	Kd3
21. Rb8	Kc6	**28.** Rb6 +	Kd5	**35.** Rxc3 +	Kxc3
22. Bxa7	g5	**29.** a5	f5	**36.** Be5	(1–0)

GAME 19

1. d4	Nf6	**13.** Nf3	Nxf3 +	**25.** b4	cxb4
2. c4	e6	**14.** Bxf3	h6	**26.** Qb2 +	Qe5
3. Nc3	c5	**15.** Bd2	a6	**27.** Qxb4	Nf4
4. d5	exd5	**16.** Be2	Qe7	**28.** Rd1	b6
5. cxd5	d6	**17.** Rae1	Qe5	**29.** Rf2	Nd3
6. Nf3	g6	**18.** Kh1	Qd4	**30.** Qxb6	Nxf2 +
7. e4	Bg7	**19.** f3	Nh5	**31.** Qxf2	Rxa4
8. Be2	O-O	**20.** Nb5	axb5	**32.** Kg1	Ra1
9. O-O	Re8	**21.** Bxb5	Qe5	**33.** Qe1	Ra2
10. Nd2	Nbd7	**22.** Bc3	Qe7	**34.** Qg3	Qb2
11. a4	Ne5	**23.** Bxe8	Qxe8	**35.** h4	Ra1
12. Qc2	g5	**24.** Bxg7	Kxg7		(0–1)

GAME 20

1. d4	Nf6	**7.** Bd3	dxc4	**13.** Ng3	Bb7
2. c4	e6	**8.** Bxc4	Qc7	**14.** Rc1	Qc6
3. Nc3	Bb4	**9.** Bb3	b6	**15.** f3	Qb5
4. e3	d5	**10.** Ne2	O-O	**16.** Ba4	Qxb2
5. a3	Bxc3 +	**11.** Bb2	Nc6		(0–1)
6. bxc3	c5	**12.** O-O	Na5		

GAME 21

1. d4	Nf6	**17.** dxe5	f6	**33.** e4	Qc6
2. c4	g6	**18.** Rb2	Be6	**34.** Rd7	Qxe4
3. Nc3	d5	**19.** Rd2	Qc7	**35.** h3	a4
4. Bg5	Ne4	**20.** Bg4	Qc8	**36.** Bf2	Kf8
5. Bh4	Nxc3	**21.** Bf3	Rb8	**37.** c4	a3
6. bxc3	dxc4	**22.** Qe2	Rd8	**38.** Qxa3	Ra8
7. e3	Be6	**23.** Rfd1	Rxd2	**39.** Qb2	Ke8
8. Rb1	b6	**24.** Qxd2	Qe8	**40.** Qb5	Kf8
9. Be2	Bh6	**25.** exf6	exf6	**41.** Rd1	Qxf4
10. Nf3	c6	**26.** Qd6	Rc8	**42.** Bxc5	Bxc5 +
11. Ne5	Bg7	**27.** a5	Bf8	**43.** Qxc5 +	Kg7
12. f4	Bd5	**28.** Qd2	Be7	**44.** Rf1	Qe4
13. O-O	Nd7	**29.** Bd5	Qf7	**45.** Qc7 +	Kh6
14. Nxc4	O-O	**30.** Bxe6	Qxe6	**46.** Rxf6	Qd4 +
15. a4	c5	**31.** Qd7	Kf7		(0–1)
16. Ne5	Nxe5	**32.** Qxa7	bxa5		

GAME 22

1. c4	c5	20. Nxe4	Qxe4	39. Bxf7	Rxh4+
2. Nf3	g6	21. Bd3	Qd4+	40. Kg2	Kxg5
3. d4	cxd4	22. Kh1	Rce8	41. Bd5	Ba6
4. Nxd4	Nc6	23. Be3	Qc3	42. Rd1	Ra4
5. e4	Nf6	24. Bxh6	Qxd2	43. Bf3	Rxa3
6. Nc3	d6	25. Bxd2	Be5	44. Rxd6	Ra2+
7. Be2	Nxd4	26. Bf4	Bxf4	45. Kg1	Kf4
8. Qxd4	Bg7	27. Rxf4	gxf5	46. Bg2	Rb2
9. Bg5	h6	28. Rxf5	Kg7	47. Rd7	b6
10. Be3	O-O	29. Rg5+	Kh6	48. Rd8	Be2
11. Qd2	Kh7	30. h4	e6	49. Bh3	Bg4
12. O-O	Be6	31. Rf1	f5	50. Bf1	Bf3
13. f4	Rc8	32. Rb1	Rf7	51. Rb8	Be4
14. b3	Qa5	33. b5	axb5	52. Ba6	Ke3
15. a3	a6	34. cxb5	Bd7	53. Rc8	Rb1+
16. f5	Bd7	35. g4	Ra8	54. Kh2	Kf4
17. b4	Qe6	36. gxf5	exf5		(0–1)
18. Rae1	Bc6	37. Bc4	Ra4		
19. Bf4	Nxe4	38. Rc1	Bxb5		

GAME 23

1. e4	e5	11. Nd2	Ne7	21. Rxg7	Rxh2
2. Nf3	Nc6	12. Nc4	O-O-O	22. a3	Bd6
3. Bb5	a6	13. Rd3	b5	23. f4!	exf4
4. Bxc6	dxc6	14. Na5	Bb4	24. d4	Kd8
5. O-O	f6	15. Nb3	Rxd3	25. Na5	c5
6. d4	Bg4	16. cxd3	Ng6	26. e5	Bf8
7. dxe5	Qxd1	17. Kf1	Rf8	27. Nc6+	Ke8
8. Rxd1	Bxf3	18. Ke2	Nf4+	28. Rxc7	(1–0)
9. gxf3	fxe5	19. Bxf4	Rxf4		
10. Be3	Bd6	20. Rg1	Rh4		

GAME 24

1. Nf3	c5	18. Ne1	g6	35. Rxc8	Rxc8
2. b3	d5	19. cxb5	axb5	36. a5	Ra8
3. Bb2	f6	20. Bb2	Nb6	37. a6	Ra7
4. c4	d4	21. Nef3	Ra8	38. Kf1	g5
5. d3	e5	22. a3	Na5	39. Ke2	Kd6
6. e3	Ne7	23. Qd1	Qf7	40. Kd3	Kc5
7. Be2	Nec6	24. a4	bxa4	41. Ng1	Kb5
8. Nbd2	Be7	25. bxa4	c4	42. Ne2	Ba5
9. O-O	O-O	26. dxc4	Naxc4	43. Rb2+	Kxa6
10. e4	a6	27. Nxc4	Nxc4	44. Rb1	Rc7
11. Ne1	b5	28. Qe2	Nxb2	45. Rb2	Be1
12. Bg4	Bxg4	29. Qxb2	Rfb8	46. f3	Ka5
13. Qxg4	Qc8	30. Qa2	Bb4	47. Rc2	Rb7
14. Qe2	Nd7	31. Qxf7+	Kxf7	48. Ra2+	Kb5
15. Nc2	Rb8	32. Rc7+	Ke6	49. Rb2+	Bb4
16. Rfc1	Qe8	33. g4	Bc3	50. Ra2	Rc7
17. Ba3	Bd6	34. Ra2	Rc8	51. Ra1	Rc8

52. Ra7	Ba5	57. Ne2	Kb3	62. Ke3	Bc5 +
53. Rd7	Bb6	58. Rb7	Ra8	63. Ke2	Rh1
54. Rd5 +	Bc5	59. Rxh7	Ra1	64. h4	Kc4
55. Nc1	Ka4	60. Nxd4 +	exd4	65. h5	Rh2 +
56. Rd7	Bb4	61. Kxd4	Rd1 +	66. Ke1	Kd3
					(0–1)

GAME 25

1. e4	e5	8. Nxd5	Bd6	15. Nf6 +	Kh8
2. f4	exf4	9. d4	g5	16. Qh5	Rd8
3. Bc4	d5	10. Nxg5	Qxg5	17. Qxh3	Na6
4. Bxd5	Nf6	11. e5	Bh3	18. Rf3	Qg6
5. Nc3	Bb4	12. Rf2	Bxe5	19. Rc1	Kg7
6. Nf3	O-O	13. dxe5	c6	20. Rg3	Rh8
7. O-O	Nxd5	14. Bxf4	Qg7	21. Qh6 mate	(1–0)

GAME 26

1. e4	c5	15. Bc4	Rhg8	29. Re3	Nc2
2. Nf3	e6	16. Rd1	Bf5	30. Rh3	Rxe5
3. d4	cxd4	17. Bd3	Bxd3	31. Nf3	Rxd5
4. Nxd4	Nc6	18. Qxd3	Nd4	32. Rxh7	Rxd3
5. Nb5	d6	19. O-O	Kb8	33. h4	Ne3
6. Bf4	e5	20. Kh1	Qxa3	34. Rxf7	Rd1 +
7. Be3	Nf6	21. f4	Rc8	35. Kh2	Ra1
8. Bg5	Be6	22. Ne4	Qxd3	36. h5	f4
9. N1c3	a6	23. cxd3	Rc2	37. Rxf4	Rxa2
10. Bxf6	gxf6	24. Rd2	Rxd2	38. Re4	Nxg2
11. Na3	d5	25. Nxd2	f5	39. Kg3	Ra5
12. exd5	Bxa3	26. fxe5	Re8	40. Ne5	(1–0)
13. bxa3	Qa5	27. Re1	Nc2		
14. Qd2	O-O-O	28. Re2	Nd4		

GAME 27

1. e4	e5	12. Bg5	a6	23. dxe5	Be7
2. Nf3	Nc6	13. Ba4	Bd7	24. Rxe7 +	Kxe7
3. Bb5	f5	14. Bxf6	gxf6	25. Qb7 +	Ke6
4. Nc3	fxe4	15. Qxe4 +	Kf7	26. Qd7 +	Kxe5
5. Nxe4	d5	16. Ne5 +	fxe5	27. Qd5 +	Kf6
6. Nxe5	dxe4	17. Rf1 +	Ke7	28. Rf1 +	Kg6
7. Nxc6	Qg5	18. Bxd7	Kxd7	29. Qe6 +	Kg5
8. Qe2	Nf6	19. Rf7 +	Ke8	30. Rf5 +	Kg4
9. f4	Qxf4	20. Rxc7	Bd6	31. Rf4 + +	Kxg3
10. d4	Qh4 +	21. Rxb7	Rc8	32. Qg4 mate	(1–0)
11. g3	Qh3	22. O-O-O	Qxh2		

GAME 28

1. e4	e5	11. Be3	Nd7	21. Bb5	Rxb5
2. Nf3	Nf6	12. O-O-O	O-O	22. Nxa4	Rb4
3. d4	exd4	13. g4	Bb4	23. Nc3	Bb7
4. e5	Ne4	14. Ne2	Nb6	24. Rhe1	Kh8
5. Qe2	Nc5	15. Nd4	Qe8	25. f6	Bd8
6. Nxd4	Nc6	16. c3	Be7	26. Bg5	Rd4
7. Nxc6	bxc6	17. f5	c5	27. fxg7+	Kxg7
8. Nc3	Rb8	18. Nb5	d4	28. Bf6+	Kg8
9. f4	Be7	19. Bf4	dxc3	29. Qh4	Rxd1+
10. Qf2	d5	20. Nxc3	Na4	30. Nxd1	(1–0)

GAME 29

1. c4	c5	17. Rb5	Qe7	33. Nc6	Qc3
2. Nf3	Nc6	18. a4	Be6	34. Rb1	Qc2
3. d4	cxd4	19. Qa1	Qf6	35. Ne7+	Kh8
4. Nxd4	Nf6	20. Kg2	Na5	36. Nxd5	Rc8
5. Nc3	e6	21. Nd4	Nb7	37. Nc3	Rxc3
6. e3	d5	22. Rb4	Nd6	38. Qxh5+	Kg8
7. cxd5	exd5	23. a5	Ne4	39. Rb8+	Rc8
8. Be2	Bd6	24. axb6	axb6	40. Rxc8+	Bxc8
9. O-O	O-O	25. Qb2	Nxc3	41. Kf1	Ba6+
10. Nf3	Bg4	26. Ba6	Rc5	42. Ke1	Qc3+
11. g3	Bb4	27. Kg1	Bh3	43. Kd1	Qd3+
12. Bd2	Ne4	28. Ra1	b5	44. Kc1	Qc3+
13. a3	Bxc3	29. Bxb5	Nxb5	45. Kd1	Bc4
14. Bxc3	Nxc3	30. Rxb5	Rxb5	46. Qf3	Bb3+
15. bxc3	Rc8	31. Qxb5	Qe5	47. Ke2	Qc4+
16. Rb1	b6	32. Re1	h5		(0–1)

GAME 30

1. e4	e6	11. h5	h6	21. Nf4	Ke7
2. d4	d5	12. Rh4	Ba6	22. Nxd5+	Kd8
3. Nc3	Bb4	13. Bxa6	Nxa6	23. Ne3	Nxe3
4. e5	c5	14. Rf4	Qd7	24. Bxe3	Rc7
5. a3	Bxc3+	15. Qf3	Nc6	25. dxc5	Nxc5
6. bxc3	Qa5	16. Nh3	Rc8	26. Rd1+	Ke7
7. Bd2	Qa4	17. g4	Qe8	27. Bxc5+	bxc5
8. Qg4	Kf8	18. g5	Ne7	28. Rxe6+	(1–0)
9. Qd1	b6	19. gxh6	gxh6		
10. h4	Ne7	20. Rf6	Nf5		

GAME 31

1. e4	c6	5. Qxf3	Nf6	9. Nb1	Qb6
2. Nc3	d5	6. d3	e6	10. b3	a5
3. Nf3	Bg4	7. g3	Bb4	11. a3	Bxd2+
4. h3	Bxf3	8. Bd2	d4	12. Nxd2	Qc5

13. Qd1	h5	22. bxa5	Rxa5	31. Qf4	Ra8
14. h4	Nbd7	23. Rfb1	b5	32. Rh1	Rg8
15. Bg2	Ng4	24. Nf3	Ra4	33. a4	bxa4
16. O-O	g5	25. Bh3	Nxf3+	34. Rb1	e5
17. b4	Qe7	26. Qxf3	Kd7	35. Rb7+	Kd6
18. Nf3	gxh4	27. Kg2	Qg7	36. Rxg7	exf4
19. Nxh4	Nde5	28. Rb4	Rga8	37. Rxg8	f3+
20. Qd2	Rg8	29. Rxa4	Rxa4	38. Kg1	Kc5
21. Qf4	f6	30. Bxg4	hxg4	39. Rb8	(1–0)

GAME 32

1. d4	Nf6	13. Nxe4	Rxe4	25. Be2	Bxf4+
2. c4	c5	14. Bg5	Qe8	26. Bxf4	Rxf4
3. d5	e6	15. Bd3	Bxf3	27. Rb6	Rxf1
4. Nc3	exd5	16. Qxf3	Rb4	28. Bxf1	Rd8
5. cxd5	d6	17. Rae1	Be5	29. Rxa6	Kg7
6. e4	g6	18. Qd1	Qxa4	30. Bb5	Kf6
7. Bf4	a6	19. Qxa4	Rxa4	31. Bc6	Ke5
8. a4	Bg7	20. f4	Bd4+	32. Ra7	Rf8
9. Nf3	O-O	21. Kh1	Nd7	33. Re7+	Kd4
10. Be2	Bg4	22. Re7	Nf6	34. Rd7	Nf6
11. O-O	Re8	23. Rxb7	Nh5	(0–1)	
12. h3	Nxe4	24. Kh2	Be3		

GAME 33

1. e4	c5	10. Kh1	Na5	19. Nh5	f5
2. Nf3	Nc6	11. Bg5	Qc5	20. Rad1	Qe5
3. d4	cxd4	12. f4	b5	21. Nef6+	Bxf6
4. Nxd4	Nf6	13. Ng3	b4	22. Nxf6+	Qxf6
5. Nc3	d6	14. e5	dxe5	23. Qxf6	Nc5
6. Bc4	Qb6	15. Bxf6	gxf6	24. Qg5+	Kh8
7. Nde2	e6	16. Nce4	Qd4	25. Qe7	Ba6
8. O-O	Be7	17. Qh5	Nxb3	26. Qxc5	Bxf1
9. Bb3	O-O	18. Qh6	exf4	27. Rxf1	(1–0)

GAME 34

1. e4	e5	15. Bf4	Bxf4	29. Re2	Bc8
2. Nf3	Nc6	16. Rxf4	Bd7	30. Qc4+	Kh7
3. Bb5	a6	17. Re1	Qc5	31. Ng6	Rxe2
4. Bxc6	dxc6	18. c3	Rae8	32. Qxe2	Bd7
5. O-O	f6	19. g4	Qd6	33. Qe7	Qxe7
6. d4	exd4	20. Qg3	Re7	34. Nxe7	g5
7. Nxd4	Ne7	21. Nf3	c5	35. hxg5	hxg5
8. Be3	Ng6	22. e5	fxe5	36. Nd5	Bc6
9. Nd2	Bd6	23. Rfe4	Bc6	37. Nxc7	Bf3
10. Nc4	O-O	24. Rxe5	Rfe8	38. Ne8	Kh6
11. Qd3	Ne5	25. Rxe7	Rxe7	39. Nf6	Kg7
12. Nxe5	Bxe5	26. Ne5	h6	40. Kf2	Bd1
13. f4	Bd6	27. h4	Bd7	41. Nd7	c4
14. f5	Qe7	28. Qf4	Qf6	42. Kg3	(1–0)

GAME 35

1. d4	Nf6	16. Nc4	b5	31. Bc6	Nxc6
2. c4	g6	17. Nd2	Qb6	32. Rc1	Qa7
3. g3	Bg7	18. Bb2	f5	33. Qxa7	Nxa7
4. Bg2	O-O	19. Ra3	Bh6	34. Rc7	Nb5
5. Nc3	d6	20. e3	Rac8	35. Rb7	Nc3
6. Nf3	Nc6	21. axb5	axb5	36. Nc4	Kf6
7. O-O	e5	22. Qa2	Bg7	37. b5	Ne5
8. d5	Ne7	23. Ra1	e4	38. Nxd6	Rd8
9. c5	Nd7	24. Bf1	Nd8	39. Rb6	Kg5
10. cxd6	cxd6	25. Ra6	Qb8	40. Ra6	Nxd5
11. a4	Nc5	26. Ra7	Rc7	41. b6	Nb4
12. Nd2	b6	27. Rxc7	Qxc7	42. Ra4	Rxd6
13. b4	Nb7	28. Nxb5	Bxb5	43. Rxb4	Rd1 +
14. Qb3	Bd7	29. Bxb5	Nf7	44. Kg2	Nf3
15. Ba3	a6	30. Bxg7	Kxg7	(0–1)	

GAME 36

1. d4	Nf6	11. Be2	Be6	21. Rfc1	Qa6
2. c4	g6	12. Nd5	b5	22. Rxc8 +	Rxc8
3. Nc3	Bg7	13. cxb5	axb5	23. Nc3	Bc4
4. e4	d6	14. Bxb5	Nxd5	24. f4	d5
5. f3	O-O	15. exd5	Bxd5	25. Bd4	Bxd4 +
6. Be3	Nbd7	16. a4	e6	26. Qxd4	Qb7
7. Qd2	c5	17. O-O	Qh4	27. Qf2	Ba6
8. Nge2	a6	18. Ne2	Rfc8	28. Rd1	Rc4
9. Ng3	cxd4	19. Be3	Nc4	29. Rd2	Rxc3
10. Bxd4	Ne5	20. Bxc4	Qxc4	(0–1)	

GAME 37

1. e4	c6	14. Be3	c5	27. Qa4	Rb7
2. d3	d5	15. a5	e5	28. Bb5	Nb8
3. Nd2	g6	16. Nd2	Ne8	29. Ra8	Bd6
4. Ngf3	Bg7	17. axb6	axb6	30. Qd1	Nc6
5. g3	Nf6	18. Nb1	Qb7	31. Qd2	h5
6. Bg2	O-O	19. Nc3	Nc7	32. Bh6 +	Kh7
7. O-O	Bg4	20. Nb5	Qc6	33. Bg5	Rb8
8. h3	Bxf3	21. Nxc7	Qxc7	34. Rxb8	Nxb8
9. Qxf3	Nbd7	22. Qb5	Ra8	35. Bf6	Nc6
10. Qe2	dxe4	23. c3	Rxa1	36. Qd5	Na7
11. dxe4	Qc7	24. Rxa1	Rb8	37. Be8	Kg8
12. a4	Rad8	25. Ra6	Bf8	38. Bxf7 +	Qxf7
13. Nb3	b6	26. Bf1	Kg7	39. Qxd6	(1–0)

GAME 38

1.	e4	e5	12.	Rxd1	Re8	23.	Kg2	cxd5
2.	Nf3	Nc6	13.	f3	Ne7	24.	exd5	Kb8
3.	Bb5	a6	14.	Nc3	Kc8	25.	Re1	Bf8
4.	Bxc6	dxc6	15.	Be3	f5	26.	Rf1	Rg7
5.	O-O	f6	16.	Rac1	fxe4	27.	Bf6	Rg8
6.	d4	Bg4	17.	fxe4	g6	28.	Rce1	Rd7
7.	c3	exd4	18.	Bf4	Bg7	29.	d6	cxd6
8.	cxd4	Qd7	19.	d5	Rd8	30.	Bxe7	Bxe7
9.	h3	Bh5	20.	Na4	Rhf8	31.	Rf7	(1–0)
10.	Ne5	Bxd1	21.	g3	g5			
11.	Nxd7	Kxd7	22.	Bxg5	Rf7			

GAME 39

1.	d4	Nf6	11.	O-O	Ncxe5	21.	Bd3	Re1 +
2.	Nf3	d5	12.	Nxe5	Nxe5	22.	Kh2	Qg1 +
3.	e3	g6	13.	Be2	c6	23.	Kg3	Rfe8
4.	c4	Bg7	14.	f4	Ng4	24.	Rb1	gxf5
5.	Nc3	O-O	15.	h3	Bf5	25.	Bd2	Rxb1
6.	Qb3	e6	16.	e4	Qd4 +	◇26.	Qxb1	Qxb1
7.	Be2	Nc6	17.	Kh1	Nf2 +	27.	Bxb1	Re2
8.	Qc2	dxc4	18.	Rxf2	Qxf2		(0–1)	
9.	Bxc4	e5	19.	exf5	Bxc3			
10.	dxe5	Ng4	20.	bxc3	Rae8			

GAME 40

1.	e4	e6	11.	O-O	c4	21.	f5	Nd8
2.	d4	d5	12.	Be2	f6	22.	Re3	Qf4
3.	Nc3	Bb4	13.	Ba3	fxe5	23.	Rf3	Qe4
4.	e5	c5	14.	dxe5	Nxe5	24.	a5	Nc6
5.	a3	Bxc3 +	15.	Re1	N7c6	25.	axb6	axb6
6.	bxc3	Ne7	16.	Nxe5	Nxe5	26.	Qb1	Kc7
7.	a4	Qc7	17.	f4	Nc6	27.	Bc1	Qe1 +
8.	Nf3	b6	18.	Bg4	O-O-O	28.	Rf1	Qxc3
9.	Bb5 +	Bd7	19.	Bxe6	Bxe6	29.	Bf4 +	Kb7
10.	Bd3	Nbc6	20.	Rxe6	Rd7	30.	Qb5	(1–0)

GAME 41

1.	e4	e5	9.	d4	Bxe4	17.	Nxd6	cxd6
2.	Nf3	Nc6	10.	Nbd2	Bg6	18.	Bf4	d5
3.	Bb5	a6	11.	Bxc6 +	bxc6	19.	Qb3	hxg4
4.	Ba4	d6	12.	dxe5	dxe5	20.	Qb7	gxh3 +
5.	O-O	Bg4	13.	Nxe5	Bd6	21.	Bg3	Rd8
6.	h3	Bh5	14.	Nxg6	Qxg6	22.	Qb4 +	(1–0)
7.	c3	Qf6	15.	Re1 +	Kf8			
8.	g4	Bg6	16.	Nc4	h5			

GAME 42

1. d4	d5	13. Kb1	O-O-O	25. Nf3	Qf6
2. c4	e6	14. Na4	Kb8	26. Bxf5	fxe3
3. Nc3	Nf6	15. Nc5	Bc8	27. Bxe6	Nxe6
4. cxd5	exd5	16. Nc1	Ng7	28. Qc3	c5
5. Bg5	c6	17. N1b3	b6	29. Rd1	cxd4
6. Qc2	Na6	18. Na4	Bb7	30. Nxd4	Nxd4
7. e3	Nc7	19. Rhe1	Nge6	31. Qxd4	Qg6 +
8. Bd3	Be7	20. Rc1	Rhe8	32. Rc2	Re4
9. Nge2	Nh5	21. a3	f5	33. Qc3	Rc8
10. Bxe7	Qxe7	22. f4	Qh4	34. Qb3	Rxc2
11. O-O-O	g6	23. Re2	g5		(0–1)
12. h3	Bd7	24. Nd2	gxf4		

GAME 43

1. e4	c5	9. Rb1	Qa3	17. Rxf8 +	Bxf8
2. Nf3	d6	10. e5	dxe5	18. Qf4	Nc6
3. d4	cxd4	11. fxe5	Nfd7	19. Qf7	Qc5 +
4. Nxd4	Nf6	12. Bc4	Bb4	20. Kh1	Nf6
5. Nc3	a6	13. Rb3	Qa5	21. Bxc8	Nxe5
6. Bg5	e6	14. O-O	O-O	22. Qe6	Neg4
7. f4	Qb6	15. Nxe6	fxe6		(0–1)
8. Qd2	Qxb2	16. Bxe6 +	Kh8		

GAME 44

1. e4	e5	15. Ne3	Rd8	29. Nf6 +	Kh8
2. Nf3	Nc6	16. Qe2	Be6	30. Nd5	Qd7
3. Bb5	a6	17. Nd5	Nxd5	31. Qe4	Qd6
4. Ba4	Nf6	18. exd5	Bxd5	32. Nf4	Re7
5. O-O	Be7	19. Nxe5	Ra7	33. Bg5	Re8
6. Re1	b5	20. Bf4	Qb6	34. Bxd8	Rxd8
7. Bb3	d6	21. Rad1	g6	35. Nxe6	Qxe6
8. c3	O-O	22. Ng4	Nc4	36. Qxe6	fxe6
9. h3	Na5	23. Bh6	Be6	37. Rxe6	Rd1 +
10. Bc2	c5	24. Bb3	Qb8	38. Kh2	Rd2
11. d4	Nd7	25. Rxd8 +	Bxd8	39. Rb6	Rxf2
12. dxc5	dxc5	26. Bxc4	bxc4	40. Rb7	Rf6
13. Nbd2	Qc7	27. Qxc4	Qd6	41. Kg3	(1–0)
14. Nf1	Nb6	28. Qa4	Qe7		

GAME 45

1. e4	c5	12. O-O-O	b5	23. g6	e5
2. Nf3	d6	13. Kb1	b4	24. gxf7 +	Kf8
3. d4	cxd4	14. Nd5	Bxd5	25. Be3	d5
4. Nxd4	Nf6	15. Bxd5	Rac8	26. exd5	Rxf7
5. Nc3	g6	16. Bb3	Rc7	27. d6	Rf6
6. Be3	Bg7	17. h4	Qb5	28. Bg5	Qb7
7. f3	O-O	18. h5	Rfc8	29. Bxf6	Bxf6
8. Qd2	Nc6	19. hxg6	hxg6	30. d7	Rd8
9. Bc4	Nxd4	20. g4	a5	31. Qd6 +	(1–0)
10. Bxd4	Be6	21. g5	Nh5		
11. Bb3	Qa5	22. Rxh5	gxh5		

GAME 46

1. e4	e6	12. Bf4	a4	23. Bf6	Qe8
2. d3	d5	13. a3	bxa3	24. Ne4	g6
3. Nd2	Nf6	14. bxa3	Na5	25. Qg5	Nxe4
4. g3	c5	15. Ne3	Ba6	26. Rxe4	c4
5. Bg2	Nc6	16. Bh3	d4	27. h5	cxd3
6. Ngf3	Be7	17. Nf1	Nb6	28. Rh4	Ra7
7. O-O	O-O	18. Ng5	Nd5	29. Bg2	dxc2
8. e5	Nd7	19. Bd2	Bxg5	30. Qh6	Qf8
9. Re1	b5	20. Bxg5	Qd7	31. Qxh7 +	(1—0)
10. Nf1	b4	21. Qh5	Rfc8		
11. h4	a5	22. Nd2	Nc3		

GAME 47

1. e4	c5	12. O-O-O	Nc4	23. Qd3	Bxc3
2. Nf3	Nc6	13. Qe2	Nxe3	24. Nxc3	Nxf4
3. d4	cxd4	14. Qxe3	O-O	25. Qf3	Nh5
4. Nxd4	Nf6	15. g4	Qa5	26. Rxh5	gxh5
5. Nc3	d6	16. h4	e6	27. Qxh5	Be8
6. Bc4	Bd7	17. Nde2	Rc6	28. Qh6	Rxc3
7. Bb3	g6	18. g5	hxg5	29. bxc3	Rxc3
8. f3	Na5	19. hxg5	Nh5	30. g6	fxg6
9. Bg5	Bg7	20. f4	Rfc8	31. Rh1	Qd4
10. Qd2	h6	21. Kb1	Qb6	32. Qh7 +	(1—0)
11. Be3	Rc8	22. Qf3	Rc5		

GAME 48

1. e4	c5	25. Bf1	a5	49. Be8 +	Kb7
2. Nf3	Nc6	26. Bc4	Rf8	50. Kb5	Nc8
3. d4	cxd4	27. Kg2	Kd6	51. Bc6 +	Kc7
4. Nxd4	Qc7	28. Kf3	Nd7	52. Bd5	Ne7
5. Nc3	e6	29. Re3	Nb8	53. Bf7	Kb7
6. g3	a6	30. Rd3 +	Kc7	54. Bb3	Ka7
7. Bg2	Nf6	31. c3	Nc6	55. Bd1	Kb7
8. O-O	Nxd4	32. Re3	Kd6	56. Bf3 +	Kc7
9. Qxd4	Bc5	33. a4	Ne7	57. Ka6	Ng8
10. Bf4	d6	34. h3	Nc6	58. Bd5	Ne7
11. Qd2	h6	35. h4	h5	59. Bc4	Nc6
12. Rad1	e5	36. Rd3 +	Kc7	60. Bf7	Ne7
13. Be3	Bg4	37. Rd5	f5	61. Be8	Kd8
14. Bxc5	dxc5	38. Rd2	Rf6	62. Bxg6	Nxg6
15. f3	Be6	39. Re2	Kd7	63. Kxb6	Kd7
16. f4	Rd8	40. Re3	g6	64. Kxc5	Ne7
17. Nd5	Bxd5	41. Bb5	Rd6	65. b4	axb4
18. exd5	e4	42. Ke2	Kd8	66. cxb4	Nc8
19. Rfe1	Rxd5	43. Rd3	Kc7	67. a5	Nd6
20. Rxe4 +	Kd8	44. Rxd6	Kxd6	68. b5	Ne4 +
21. Qe2	Rxd1 +	45. Kd3	Ne7	69. Kb6	Kc8
22. Qxd1 +	Qd7	46. Be8	Kd5	70. Kc6	Kb8
23. Qxd7 +	Kxd7	47. Bf7 +	Kd6	71. b6	(1—0)
24. Re5	b6	48. Kc4	Kc6		

GAME 49

1. d4	Nf6	**12.** f5	exf5	**23.** c4	Rbe8		
2. c4	c5	**13.** Nxf5	Bxf5	**24.** cxb5	axb5		
3. Nf3	cxd4	**14.** Qxf5	Nd7	**25.** Kh1	Qe7		
4. Nxd4	e6	**15.** Bf3	Qc7	**26.** Qxb5	Rxe4		
5. Nc3	Bb4	**16.** Rb1	Rab8	**27.** Rxe4	Qxe4		
6. e3	Ne4	**17.** Bd5	Nf6	**28.** Qd7	Qf4		
7. Qc2	Nxc3	**18.** Ba3	Rfe8	**29.** Kg1	Qd4+		
8. bxc3	Be7	**19.** Qd3	Nxd5	**30.** Kh1	Qf2		
9. Be2	O-O	**20.** cxd5	b5	(0–1)			
10. O-O	a6	**21.** e4	Bf8				
11. f4	d6	**22.** Rb4	Re5				

GAME 50

1. d4	Nf6	**15.** Ng3	c4	**29.** Kxg2	Bg4		
2. c4	c5	**16.** O-O	Rb8	**30.** Nf5	Nf4+		
3. d5	e6	**17.** Qa4	Qxa4	**31.** Kg3	Bxf5		
4. Nc3	exd5	**18.** Bxa4	Nd3	**32.** exf5	Bxc3		
5. cxd5	d6	**19.** Bb5	Ng4	**33.** Kf3	Be5		
6. Nf3	g6	**20.** Nge2	Nxc1	**34.** Ke4	Rb4+		
7. e4	Bg7	**21.** Raxc1	Ne5	**35.** Rc4	Rfb8		
8. Bg5	h6	**22.** b3	cxb3	**36.** f6	Kf7		
9. Bf4	g5	**23.** axb3	a6	**37.** Kf5	Rxc4		
10. Bc1	O-O	**24.** Ba4	Nd3	**38.** bxc4	Ne2		
11. Nd2	Nbd7	**25.** Rc2	f5	**39.** Re1	Nd4+		
12. Be2	Ne5	**26.** Ng3	f4	**40.** Kg4	h5+		
13. Nf1	b5	**27.** Nge2	f3	**41.** Kh3	Kxf6		
14. Bxb5	Qa5	**28.** Ng3	fxg2	(0–1)			

GAME 51

1. Nc3	c5	**14.** Re1	b4	**27.** Nd2	h4		
2. Nf3	Nf6	**15.** Na4	Rd8	**28.** Nbc4	hxg3+		
3. e4	d6	**16.** Nd2	Nd4	**29.** fxg3	Qe6		
4. g3	g6	**17.** Nc4	Nd5	**30.** Ne4	f5		
5. Bg2	Bg7	**18.** Bxd4	exd4	**31.** Qa5	Ra8		
6. O-O	Nc6	**19.** b3	Bb7	**32.** Qxa8+	Bxa8		
7. d3	O-O	**20.** Qd2	e5	**33.** Rxa8+	Bf8		
8. h3	Rb8	**21.** Nab2	Ra8	**34.** Ned6	Qd5		
9. a4	a6	**22.** Kh2	h5	**35.** Re8	Qf3		
10. Be3	b5	**23.** Bxd5	Bxd5	**36.** h4	Qf2+		
11. axb5	axb5	**24.** Qxb4	Rxa1	**37.** Kh3	Qg1		
12. e5	dxe5	**25.** Rxa1	Qd7	(0–1)			
13. Bxc5	Qc7	**26.** Qe1	Qf5				

GAME 52

1.	d4	Nf6	11.	cxd4	b6	21.	Bb5	Qd6
2.	c4	g6	12.	Qd3	O-O	22.	Ne2	exd5
3.	Nc3	d5	13.	Bd2	Bb7	23.	exd5	Qxd5
4.	cxd5	Nxd5	14.	O-O	e6	24.	Qxd5	Bxd5
5.	e4	Nxc3	15.	Rfd1	Qd7	25.	Rxd5	Rb1+
6.	bxc3	Bg7	16.	Bxa5	bxa5	26.	Nc1	Rxc1+
7.	Bc4	Nc6	17.	Bc4	Rab8	27.	Bf1	Re8
8.	a4	Na5	18.	Ra2	Bc6	28.	f4	Ree1
9.	Ba2	c5	19.	Nc3	Rb4	29.	Rf2	Bf8
10.	Ne2	cxd4	20.	d5	Bb7		(0–1)	

GAME 53

1.	e4	c5	16.	Bd4	Re8	31.	Rxe8+	Kh7
2.	Nf3	d6	17.	Rd1	Ng4	32.	c5	Qf6
3.	d4	cxd4	18.	h3	Qh4	33.	Re1	bxc5
4.	Nxd4	Nf6	19.	Rdf1	Bxd4	34.	bxc5	Qb2
5.	Nc3	Nc6	20.	Qxd4	Rad8	35.	Rff1	Qxa2
6.	Bc4	e6	21.	Nxd5	Bxd5	36.	c6	Qa5
7.	Bb3	Be7	22.	Bxd5	Nf6	37.	Rc1	Qc7
8.	O-O	Nxd4	23.	c4	Rd7	38.	Rfd1	g5
9.	Qxd4	O-O	24.	Re3	Red8	39.	fxg5	Kg6
10.	f4	b6	25.	Qe5	h6	40.	gxh6	Kxh6
11.	Kh1	Ba6	26.	Bf3	Rd2	41.	Rd6+	Kg7
12.	Rf3	d5	27.	b4	Rf2	42.	Rd4	Kg6
13.	exd5	Bc5	28.	Ree1	Rxf3	43.	Ra4	(1–0)
14.	Qa4	Bb7	29.	Rxf3	Re8			
15.	Be3	exd5	30.	Qxe8+	Nxe8			

GAME 54

1.	d4	Nf6	9.	Be2	Bxf3	17.	Bd2	exf4
2.	c4	g6	10.	Bxf3	e5	18.	Bxf4	Ne5
3.	Nc3	Bg7	11.	d5	Ne7	19.	Bc2	Nd4
4.	e4	d6	12.	Be2	f5	20.	Qd2	Nxc4
5.	Nf3	O-O	13.	f4	h6	21.	Qf2	Rxf4
6.	Bd3	Bg4	14.	Bd3	Kh7	22.	Qxf4	Ne2+
7.	O-O	Nc6	15.	Qe2	fxe4	23.	Kh1	Nxf4
8.	Be3	Nd7	16.	Nxe4	Nf5		(0–1)	

GAME 55

1.	e4	c5	10.	Qe1	Bb7	19.	Rfd2	Nc5
2.	Nf3	d6	11.	Nh4	g6	20.	Bf1	b4
3.	d4	cxd4	12.	Nf3	Bg7	21.	Nd5	Bxd5
4.	Nxd4	Nf6	13.	Qh4	O-O	22.	exd5	Ne4
5.	Nc3	a6	14.	fxe5	dxe5	23.	Qe1	Nxd2
6.	f4	e5	15.	Bh6	Nh5	24.	Qxd2	Nxd5
7.	Nf3	Qc7	16.	Bxg7	Kxg7	25.	c4	bxc3
8.	Bd3	Nbd7	17.	Rad1	Nf4		(0–1)	
9.	O-O	b5	18.	Rf2	f6			

GAME 56

1.	d4	Nf6	13.	Bd3	f5	25.	h3	f4
2.	c4	e6	14.	Qxa8	Nc6	26.	Kh2	a6
3.	Nc3	Bb4	15.	Qxe8+	Qxe8	27.	Re4	Qd5
4.	e3	b6	16.	O-O	Na5	28.	h4	Ne3
5.	Ne2	Ba6	17.	Rae1	Bxc4	29.	R1xe3	fxe3
6.	Ng3	Bxc3+	18.	Bxc4	Nxc4	30.	Rxe3	Qxa2
7.	bxc3	d5	19.	Bc1	c5	31.	Rf3+	Ke8
8.	Qf3	O-O	20.	dxc5	bxc5	32.	Bg7	Qc4
9.	e4	dxe4	21.	Bf4	h6	33.	hxg5	hxg5
10.	Nxe4	Nxe4	22.	Re2	g5	34.	Rf8+	Kd7
11.	Qxe4	Qd7	23.	Be5	Qd8	35.	Ra8	Kc6
12.	Ba3	Re8	24.	Rfe1	Kf7		(0–1)	

GAME 57

1.	e4	c5	12.	Qe2	Qa5	23.	Rxf2	Qb6
2.	Nf3	Nc6	13.	f5	e5	24.	Rg2	d5
3.	d4	cxd4	14.	Bf2	Bd8	25.	Bxd5	Rad8
4.	Nxd4	Nf6	15.	Rad1	Bb6	26.	Qh5	g6
5.	Nc3	d6	16.	g4	h6	27.	Qxh6	Rxd5
6.	Bc4	e6	17.	h4	Nh7	28.	exd5	e4
7.	Bb3	Be7	18.	Rd3	Kh8	29.	Rdg3	Qd6
8.	O-O	O-O	19.	g5	Bd4	30.	h5	Rg8
9.	Be3	Bd7	20.	Bb5	Bb5	31.	hxg6	fxg6
10.	f4	Nxd4	21.	Nxb5	Qxb5	32.	f6	Qxd5
11.	Bxd4	Bc6	22.	c3	Bxf2	33.	Qxh7+	(1–0)

GAME 58

1.	e4	c5	10.	Qd2	Nf6	19.	Bxc6	Qxc6
2.	Nc3	d6	11.	Kh1	O-O-O	20.	Nf7	Rde8
3.	g3	Nc6	12.	Rae1	Kb8	21.	Nxe5	Rxe5
4.	Bg2	g6	13.	Bg1	fxe4	22.	Qf4	b5
5.	d3	Bg7	14.	dxe4	Ba6	23.	a3	b4
6.	f4	b6	15.	Ng5	Bxf1	24.	axb4	cxb4
7.	Nf3	Bb7	16.	Bxf1	Rhe8	25.	Bd4	Rf5
8.	O-O	Qd7	17.	Bb5	e5		(0–1)	
9.	Be3	f5	18.	fxe5	Rxe5			

GAME 59

1.	d4	Nf6	10.	Nd2	Qh4	19.	Kxf1	c5
2.	c4	e6	11.	f3	Nxd2	20.	Kg1	Ba6
3.	Nc3	Bb4	12.	Bxd2	Nc6	21.	Bg3	cxd4
4.	e3	b6	13.	Rae1	Na5	22.	cxd4	exd4
5.	Bd3	Bb7	14.	Rb1	d6	23.	Bxd6	Qe3+
6.	Nf3	Ne4	15.	Be1	Qg5	24.	Qxe3	dxe3
7.	Qc2	f5	16.	Qe2	e5	25.	Re1	Bxc4
8.	O-O	Bxc3	17.	e4	fxe4	26.	Rxe3	Bxa2
9.	bxc3	O-O	18.	fxe4	Rxf1+	27.	e5	Be6

28. Re1	Nb3	34. Kf2	Nc1	40. Kxg4	Rxg2 +
29. Ba6	Nc5	35. Re3	Rb8	41. Kh3	Rg1
30. Be2	a5	36. Bc5	Rb2 +	42. e6	Nf5
31. Bc7	a4	37. Kg3	Nb3	43. Rd3	g5
32. Bxb6	Nb3	38. Bd6	Nd4	44. Bg3	h5
33. Bd1	Rc8	39. Bg4	Bxg4	(0–1)	

GAME 60

1. d4	Nf6	10. Nh4	h6	19. Rbf2	Qe7
2. c4	e6	11. f4	Ng6	20. Bc2	g5
3. Nc3	Bb4	12. Nxg6	fxg6	21. Bd2	Qe8
4. Nf3	c5	13. fxe5	dxe5	22. Be1	Qg6
5. e3	Nc6	14. Be3	b6	23. Qd3	Nh5
6. Bd3	Bxc3 +	15. O-O	O-O	24. Rxf8 +	Rxf8
7. bxc3	d6	16. a4	a5	25. Rxf8 +	Kxf8
8. e4	e5	17. Rb1	Bd7	26. Bd1	Nf4
9. d5	Ne7	18. Kb2	Rb8	27. Qc2	Bxa4 (1–0)

GAME 61

1. e4	c5	13. Bf4	Na5	25. Rxc8 +	Nxc8
2. Nf3	e6	14. Rc1	b5	26. h5	Qd8
3. d3	Nc6	15. b3	b4	27. Ng5	Nf8
4. g3	g6	16. Ne2	Bb5	28. Be4	Qe7
5. Bg2	Bg7	17. Qd2	Nac6	29. Nxh7	Nxh7
6. O-O	Nge7	18. g4	a5	30. hxg6	fxg6
7. Re1	d6	19. Ng3	Qb6	31. Bxg6	Ng5
8. c3	O-O	20. h4	Nb8	32. Nh5	Nf3 +
9. d4	cxd4	21. Bh6	Nd7	33. Kg2	Nh4 +
10. cxd4	d5	22. Qg5	Rxc1	34. Kg3	Nxg6
11. e5	Bd7	23. Rxc1	Bxh6	35. Nf6 +	Kf7
12. Nc3	Rc8	24. Qxh6	Rc8	36. Qh7 +	(1–0)

GAME 62

1. d4	Nf6	9. O-O	b6	17. Kg1	Nxe3
2. c4	g6	10. b3	Ba6	18. Qd2	Nxg2
3. g3	c6	11. Ba3	Re8	19. Kxg2	d4
4. Bg2	d5	12. Qd2	e5	20. Nxd4	Bb7 +
5. cxd5	cxd5	13. dxe5	Nxe5	21. Kf1	Qd7
6. Nc3	Bg7	14. Rfd1	Nd3	(0–1)	
7. e3	O-O	15. Qc2	Nxf2		
8. Nge2	Nc6	16. Kxf2	Ng4 +		

GAME 63

1. e4	e5	15. dxe5	dxe5	29. Be3	Qxa5
2. Nf3	Nc6	16. Nh2	Rad8	30. a4	Ra8
3. Bb5	a6	17. Qf3	Be6	31. axb5	Qxb5
4. Ba4	Nf6	18. Nhg4	Nxg4	32. Rhb1	Qc6
5. O-O	Be7	19. hxg4	Qc6	33. Rb6	Qc7
6. Re1	b5	20. g5	Nc4	34. Rba6	Rxa6
7. Bb3	d6	21. Ng4	Bxg4	35. Rxa6	Rc8
8. c3	O-O	22. Qxg4	Nb6	36. Qg4	Ne6
9. h3	Na5	23. g3	c4	37. Ba4	Rb8
10. Bc2	c5	24. Kg2	Nd7	38. Rc6	Qd8
11. d4	Qc7	25. Rh1	Nf8	39. Rxe6	Qc8
12. Nbd2	Bd7	26. b4	Qe6	40. Bd7	(1–0)
13. Nf1	Rfe8	27. Qe2	a5		
14. Ne3	g6	28. bxa5	Qa6		

GAME 64

1. e4	e5	14. Nf5	Bxf5	27. Rg6	Bd6
2. Nf3	Nc6	15. exf5	Qc7	28. Rag1	Bf8
3. Bb5	a6	16. g4	h6	29. h6	Qe5
4. Ba4	Nf6	17. h4	c4	30. Qg4	Rdd7
5. O-O	Be7	18. Bc2	Nh7	31. f3	Bc5
6. Re1	b5	19. Nf3	f6	32. Nxc5	Qxc5
7. Bb3	d6	20. Nd2	Rad8	33. Rxg7	Rxg7
8. c3	O-O	21. Qf3	h5	34. hxg7+	Kg8
9. h3	Nb8	22. gxh5	Nd5	35. Qg6	Rd8
10. d4	Nbd7	23. Ne4	Nf4	36. Be4	Qc8
11. Nh4	Nb6	24. Bxf4	exf4	37. Qe8+	(1–0)
12. Nd2	c5	25. Kh1	Kh8		
13. dxc5	dxc5	26. Rg1	Rf7		

GAME 65

1. e4	g6	8. Qxf3	Nc6	15. Qg3	Kh8
2. d4	Bg7	9. Be3	e5	16. Qg4	c6
3. Nc3	d6	10. dxe5	dxe5	17. Qh5	Qe8
4. f4	Nf6	11. f5	gxf5	18. Bxd4	exd4
5. Nf3	O-O	12. Qxf5	Nd4	19. Rf6	Kg8
6. Bd3	Bg4	13. Qf2	Ne8	20. e5	h6
7. h3	Bxf3	14. O-O	Nd6	21. Ne2	(1–0)

GAME 66

1. d4	Nf6	14. Nxb5	Bxb5	27. Bc1	Bd4 +
2. c4	g6	15. cxb5	Rfb8	28. Kh1	Rf2
3. g3	Bg7	16. Bf3	Nf6	29. Bg4	Nf6
4. Bg2	O-O	17. a4	a6	30. Bh3	Rc2
5. Nf3	d6	18. bxa6	Qxa6	31. a6	Ra7
6. O-O	Nc6	19. Ra3	Qxd3	32. Bc8	Nxd5
7. Nc3	Bf5	20. exd3	Rb4	33. Rb3	Nb4
8. d5	Na5	21. a5	Rb5	34. f5	gxf5
9. Nd4	Bd7	22. Bd2	Rxb2	35. Bg5	e6
10. Qd3	c5	23. Bc3	Rb7	○36. Bd8	Ra8
11. Nb3	Ng4	24. Re1	Ne8	37. Bb6	Rxc8
12. f4	b5	25. Bd2	Kf8	(0-1)	
13. Nxa5	Qxa5	26. Bd1	Rb2		

GAME 67

1. e4	e5	10. d5	b5	19. dxc6	Be6
2. Nf3	Nc6	11. Qe2	Na5	20. Qh5	Bh6
3. Bb5	a6	12. Bd1	Be7	21. Bg4	Bxg4
4. Ba4	d6	13. g3	O-O	22. Qxg4	Nxc6
5. c3	Bd7	14. h4	Rfc8	23. Rd1	b4
6. d4	Nge7	15. Bg5	hxg5	24. Nc4	bxc3
7. Bb3	h6	16. hxg5	Qxg5	25. bxc3	Nd4
8. Qe2	Ng6	17. Nxg5	Bxg5	26. Nb6	(1-0)
9. Qc4	Qf6	18. Na3	c6		

GAME 68

1. d4	Nf6	10. Ne2	Bxd5	19. b3	Qa5
2. c4	g6	11. exd5	Nbd7	20. Rc1	Qxa2
3. Nc3	Bg7	12. O-O	Ne5	♭21. Rc2	Re3
4. e4	O-O	13. f4	Nxd3	22. Qxe3	Qxc2
5. Bg5	d6	14. Qxd3	h6	23. Kh1	a5
6. Qd2	c5	15. Bh4	Re8	24. h4	a4
7. d5	e6	16. Rae1	Qb6	(0-1)	
8. Bd3	exd5	17. Bxf6	Bxf6		
9. Nxd5	Be6	18. f5	g5		

GAME 69

1. e4	c5	10. f5	Bc4	19. Qxd5	Ra4
2. Nf3	d6	11. a4	Be7	20. c3	Qa6
3. d4	cxd4	12. Be3	O-O	21. h3	Rc8
4. Nxd4	Nf6	13. a5	b5	22. Rfe1	h6
5. Nc3	a6	14. axb6	Nxb6	23. Kh2	Bg5
6. Be2	e5	15. Bxb6	Qxb6 +	24. g3	Qa7
7. Nb3	Be6	16. Kh1	Bb5	25. Kg2	Ra2
8. O-O	Nbd7	17. Bxb5	axb5	○26. Kf1	Rxc3
9. f4	Qc7	18. Nd5	Nxd5	(0-1)	

GAME 70

#	White	Black	#	White	Black	#	White	Black
1.	e4	c5	31.	Bxc3	Rxc3	61.	Bc2	Nf7 +
2.	Nf3	Nc6	32.	Kb2	d3	62.	Kg4	Ne5 +
3.	d4	cxd4	33.	Kxc3	dxe2	63.	Kf4	Kd4
4.	Nxd4	e6	34.	Re1	Nd6	64.	Rb4 +	Kc3
5.	Nb5	d6	35.	Bh5	Nb5 +	65.	Rb5	Nf7
6.	Bf4	e5	36.	Kb2	axb4	66.	Rc5 +	Kd4
7.	Be3	Nf6	37.	axb4	Rd4	67.	Rf5	g5 +
8.	Bg5	Qa5 +	38.	c3	Rh4	68.	Kg4	Ne5 +
9.	Qd2	Nxe4	39.	Bxe2	Nd6	69.	Kxg5	Rg6 +
10.	Qxa5	Nxa5	40.	Rd1	Kc7	70.	Kxh4	Rxg2
11.	Be3	Kd7	41.	h3	Rf4	71.	Bd1	Rg8
12.	N1c3	Nxc3	42.	Rf1	Re4	72.	Bg4	Ke4
13.	Nxc3	Kd8	43.	Bd3	Re5	73.	Kg3	Rg7
14.	Nb5	Be6	44.	Rf2	h5	74.	Rf4 +	Kd5
15.	O-O-O	b6	45.	c4	Rg5	75.	Ra4	Ng6
16.	f4	exf4	46.	Kc3	Kd7	76.	Ra6	Ne5
17.	Bxf4	Nb7	47.	Ra2	Kc8	77.	Kf4	Rf7 +
18.	Be2	Bd7	48.	Kd4	Kc7	78.	Kg5	Rg7 +
19.	Rd2	Be7	49.	Ra7 +	Kd8	79.	Kf5	Rf7 +
20.	Rhd1	Bxb5	50.	c5	bxc5 +	80.	Rf6	Rxf6 +
21.	Bxb5	Kc7	51.	bxc5	Ne8	81.	Kxf6	Ke4
22.	Re2	Bf6	52.	Ra2	Nc7	82.	Bc8	Kf4
23.	Rde1	Rac8	53.	Bc4	Kd7	83.	h4	Nf3
24.	Bc4	Rhf8	54.	Rb2	Kc6	84.	h5	Ng5
25.	b4	a5	55.	Bb3	Nb5 +	85.	Bf5	Nf3
26.	Bd5	Kb8	56.	Ke3	Kxc5	86.	h6	Ng5
27.	a3	Rfd8	57.	Kf4	Rg6	87.	Kg6	Nf3
28.	Bxf7	Bc3	58.	Bd1	h4	88.	h7	Ne5 +
29.	Bd2	d5	59.	Kf5	Rh6	89.	Kf6	(1–0)
30.	Rd1	d4	60.	Kg5	Nd6			

GAME 71

#	White	Black	#	White	Black	#	White	Black
1.	e4	c5	14.	Kb1	Rc8	27.	Rxg6	Nf8
2.	Nf3	e6	15.	a3	Nxd3	28.	Rg4	Rf7
3.	d4	cxd4	16.	cxd3	Nc5	29.	Qg2	Qb7
4.	Nxd4	a6	17.	Nd4	Ba8	30.	Bg5	Bxg5
5.	Nc3	Qc7	18.	f5	e5	31.	Rxg5	Rh6
6.	Bd3	Nc6	19.	Nde2	Bd8	32.	Nd4	Ne6
7.	Nb3	Nf6	20.	Rhg1	Qb8	33.	Nxe6	Rxe6
8.	Be3	d6	21.	g6	hxg6	34.	Qg4	Rh6
9.	f4	b5	22.	fxg6	Rc7	35.	Rc2	Kd8
10.	Qf3	Bb7	23.	d4	exd4	36.	Rf5	Rxf5
11.	g4	Be7	24.	Rxd4	Rd7	37.	Qxf5	Rh8
12.	O-O-O	Nb4	25.	Nd5	Ne6	38.	Qg5 +	Ke8
13.	g5	Nd7	26.	Rd2	fxg6	39.	Rc8 +	(1–0)

GAME 72

#	White	Black	#	White	Black	#	White	Black
1.	e4	e5	5.	O-O	Be7	9.	h3	h6
2.	Nf3	Nc6	6.	Re1	b5	10.	d4	Re8
3.	Bb5	a6	7.	Bb3	d6	11.	Nbd2	Bf8
4.	Ba4	Nf6	8.	c3	O-O	12.	Nf1	Bb7

13.	Ng3	Na5	21.	Qd2	Nh7	29.	f3	Nf8
14.	Bc2	Nc4	22.	Kh2	Be7	30.	h4	gxh4
15.	b3	Nb6	23.	Nf5	Bg5	31.	Rxh4	Rh7
16.	a4	c5	24.	Nxg5	hxg5	32.	Rah1	Rxh4
17.	d5	c4	25.	g4	g6	33.	Rxh4	g5
18.	b4	Bc8	26.	Ng3	f6	34.	Rh6	Kg7
19.	Be3	Bd7	27.	Rh1	Rf8	35.	Rxf6	(1–0)
20.	a5	Nc8	28.	Kg2	Rf7			

GAME 73

1.	e4	e5	13.	dxc5	dxc5	25.	Rxd1	Rd8
2.	Nf3	Nc6	14.	Nf1	Be6	26.	Rxd8+	Qxd8
3.	Bb5	a6	15.	Ne3	Rad8	27.	b3	cxb3
4.	Ba4	Nf6	16.	Qe2	c4	28.	Bxb3	Nf8
5.	O-O	Be7	17.	Nf5	Rfe8	29.	c4	Qd7
6.	Re1	b5	18.	Bg5	Nd7	30.	Qc2	Qb7
7.	Bb3	d6	19.	Bxe7	Nxe7	31.	cxb5	axb5
8.	c3	O-O	20.	Ng5	h6	32.	Ng4	N6d7
9.	h3	Na5	21.	Nxe6	fxe6	33.	Qd3	Qc6
10.	Bc2	c5	22.	Ne3	Ng6	34.	Qe3	Kf7
11.	d4	Qc7	23.	g3	Nf6	35.	Nxe5+	Nxe5
12.	Nbd2	Nc6	24.	Red1	Rxd1+	36.	Qf4+	(1–0)

GAME 74

1.	c4	g6	24.	Rxc5	Bxc5	47.	e4	a4
2.	Nc3	c5	25.	Nd3	Bxd3	48.	Kg2	Ra2
3.	g3	Bg7	26.	Qxd3	Rd8	49.	Rxf7+	Kxf7
4.	Bg2	Nc6	27.	Bf3	Qc7	50.	Bc4+	Ke7
5.	Nf3	e6	28.	Bg5	Be7	51.	Bxa2	a3
6.	O-O	Nge7	29.	Bxe7	Qxe7	52.	Kf3	Nf6
7.	d3	O-O	30.	Qd4	e5	53.	Ke3	Kd6
8.	Bd2	d5	31.	Qc4	Nb6	54.	f4	Nd7
9.	a3	b6	32.	Qc2	Rc8	55.	Bb1	Nc5
10.	Rb1	Bb7	33.	Qd3	Rc4	56.	f5	Na6
11.	b4	cxb4	34.	Bg2	Qc7	57.	g4	Nb4
12.	axb4	dxc4	35.	Qa3	Rc3	58.	fxg6	hxg6
13.	dxc4	Rc8	36.	Qa5	Rc5	59.	h5	gxh5
14.	c5	bxc5	37.	Qa3	a5	60.	gxh5	Ke6
15.	bxc5	Na5	38.	h4	Nc4	61.	Kd2	Kf6
16.	Na4	Bc6	39.	Qd3	Nd6	62.	Kc3	a2
17.	Qc2	Nb7	40.	Kh2	Kg7	63.	Bxa2	Nxa2+
18.	Rfc1	Qd7	41.	Rd1	Ne8	64.	Kb2	Nb4
19.	Ne1	Nd5	42.	Qd7	Qxd7	65.	Kc3	Nc6
20.	Nb2	Bb5	43.	Rxd7	Nf6	66.	Kc4	Nd4
21.	Ned3	Bd4	44.	Ra7	Ng4+		(0–1)	
22.	Qb3	Nxc5	45.	Kg1	Rc1+			
23.	Nxc5	Rxc5	46.	Bf1	Ra1			

GAME 75

1. d4	Nf6	9. cxd6	exd6	17. f4	Nf6
2. c4	g6	10. Ne4	Bf5	18. Be2	Rfe8
3. Nc3	Bg7	11. Ng3	Be6	19. Kf2	Rxe6
4. e4	O-O	12. Nf3	Qc7	20. Re1	Rae8
5. e5	Ne8	13. Qb1	dxe5	21. Bf3	Rxe3
6. f4	d6	14. f5	e4	22. Rxe3	Rxe3
7. Be3	c5	15. fxe6	exf3	23. Kxe3	Qxf4+
8. dxc5	Nc6	16. gxf3	f5	(0–1)	

GAME 76

1. c4	g6	12. Nf4	Nbd7	23. Kg1	Bxf4
2. Nc3	Bg7	13. a4	Nf8	24. exf4	Kg7
3. g3	e5	14. c5	d5	25. f5	Rh8
4. Bg2	d6	15. b5	N8h7	26. Bh6+	Rxh6
5. e3	Nf6	16. Bd2	Ng5	27. Rxh6	Kxh6
6. Nge2	O-O	17. Rb2	Qd7	28. Qd2+	g5
7. O-O	c6	18. Kh2	Bh6	29. bxc6	Qxf5
8. d4	Re8	19. a5	Bg4	30. Nd1	Qh3
9. Rb1	e4	20. hxg4	hxg4	31. Ne3	Kg6
10. b4	Bf5	21. Rh1	Nf3+	(0–1)	
11. h3	h5	22. Bxf3	gxf3		

GAME 77

1. e4	e5	9. c4	Nc7	17. Bxf4	Qxf4
2. f4	exf4	10. d4	O-O	18. g3	Qh6
3. Bc4	Ne7	11. Bxf4	Ne6	19. Kg1	Bh3
4. Nc3	c6	12. Be3	Bb4+	20. Ne5	Bxf1
5. Nf3	d5	13. Kf2	Nd7	21. Rxf1	Bd2
6. Bb3	dxe4	14. c5	Nf6	22. Rf3	Rad8
7. Nxe4	Nd5	15. Nxf6+	Qxf6	23. Nxf7	Rxf7
8. Qe2	Be7	16. Rhf1	Nf4	24. Qe7	(1–0)

GAME 78

1. c4	e6	15. dxc5	bxc5	29. Qg3	Re7
2. Nf3	d5	16. O-O	Ra7	30. h4	Rbb7
3. d4	Nf6	17. Be2	Nd7	31. e6	Rbc7
4. Nc3	Be7	18. Nd4	Qf8	32. Qe5	Qe8
5. Bg5	O-O	19. Nxe6	fxe6	33. a4	Qd8
6. e3	h6	20. e4	d4	34. R1f2	Qe8
7. Bh4	b6	21. f4	Qe7	35. R2f3	Qd8
8. cxd5	Nxd5	22. e5	Rb8	36. Bd3	Qe8
9. Bxe7	Qxe7	23. Bc4	Kh8	37. Qe4	Nf6
10. Nxd5	exd5	24. Qh3	Nf8	38. Rxf6	gxf6
11. Rc1	Be6	25. b3	a5	39. Rxf6	Kg8
12. Qa4	c5	26. f5	exf5	40. Bc4	Kh8
13. Qa3	Rc8	27. Rxf5	Nh7	41. Qf4	(1–0)
14. Bb5	a6	28. Rcf1	Qd8		

GAME 79

1. d4	Nf6	6. Nf3	Nc6	11. exd4	bxc6
2. c4	e6	7. O-O	dxc4	12. Bg5	Re8
3. Nc3	Bb4	8. Bxc4	Bd6	13. Qd3	c5
4. e3	O-O	9. Bb5	e5	⚲14. dxc5	Bxh2+
5. Bd3	d5	10. Bxc6	exd4		(0–1)

GAME 80

1. e4	c5	16. Bxc1	Bxb5	31. bxc3	Rxe5+
2. Nf3	d6	17. Nd5	Bh4+	32. Kd2	Rxe1
3. d4	cxd4	18. g3	Bxf1	33. Kxe1	Kd5
4. Nxd4	Nf6	19. Rxf1	Bd8	34. Kd2	Kc4
5. f3	Nc6	20. Bd2	Rc8	35. h5	b6
6. c4	e6	21. Bc3	f5	36. Kc2	g5
7. Nc3	Be7	22. e5	Rc5	37. h6	f4
8. Be3	O-O	23. Nb4	Ba5	38. g4	a5
9. Nc2	d5	24. a3	Bxb4	39. bxa5	bxa5
10. cxd5	exd5	25. axb4	Rd5	40. Kb2	a4
11. Nxd5	Nxd5	26. Ke2	Kf7	41. Ka3	Kxc3
12. Qxd5	Qc7	27. h4	Ke6	42. Kxa4	Kd4
13. Qb5	Bd7	28. Ke3	Rc8	43. Kb4	Ke3
14. Rc1	Nb4	29. Rg1	Rc4		(0–1)
15. Nxb4	Qxc1+	30. Re1	Rxc3+		

GAME 81

1. e4	e5	13. h3	Bxf3	25. Ne3	gxh3
2. Nf3	Nc6	14. Qxf3	O-O	26. g3	Bg5
3. Bb5	a6	15. Bc5	Qe6	27. Nf5	h5
4. Ba4	d6	16. Nd2	Rad8	28. Kxh3	Rd7
5. c3	Bd7	17. Bxc6	bxc6	29. Kg2	Qd8
6. d4	g6	18. Qe2	Rb8	30. Qe2	h4
7. O-O	Bg7	19. Qxa6	Bf6	31. Rxd7	Qxd7
8. Bg5	Nge7	20. b4	Rfd8	32. Qg4	Qd8
9. dxe5	dxe5	21. a4	g5	33. Rd1	Qf6
10. Qe2	h6	22. Kh2	g4	34. gxh4	Bxh4
11. Be3	Qc8	23. Qc4	Qc8	35. Be7	(1–0)
12. Rd1	Bg4	24. Nf1	Ng6		

GAME 82

1. e4	c5	9. f5	Nfxe4	17. Qe2+	Be6
2. Nf3	d6	10. fxe6	Qh4+	18. Nf4	Kd7
3. d4	cxd4	11. g3	Nxg3	19. O-O-O	Qe8
4. Nxd4	Nf6	12. Nf3	Qh5	20. Bxe6+	Nxe6
5. Nc3	a6	13. exf7+	Kd8	21. Qe4	g6
6. Bc4	e6	14. Rg1	Nf5	22. Nxe6	(1–0)
7. Bb3	Nbd7	15. Nd5	Qxf7		
8. f4	Nc5	16. Bg5+	Ke8		

GAME 83

1.	c4	g6	13.	a5	Nf6	25.	Be4	Nf5
2.	Nf3	Bg7	14.	Qa4	Bd7	26.	Rc6	Qg7
3.	d4	Nf6	15.	Qa3	Bh6	27.	Rb1	Nh4
4.	Nc3	O-O	16.	Bd3	Qc7	28.	Qd3	Bf5
5.	e4	d6	17.	bxc5	bxc5	29.	Kh1	f3
6.	Be2	e5	18.	exf5	gxf5	30.	Ng3	fxg2+
7.	O-O	Nc6	19.	Bc2	a6	31.	Kg1	Bxe4
8.	d5	Ne7	20.	Nde4	Bxc1	32.	Qxe4	Nf3+
9.	Nd2	c5	21.	Nxf6+	Rxf6	33.	Kxg2	Nd2
10.	Rb1	Ne8	22.	Rfxc1	Raf8		(0–1)	
11.	b4	b6	23.	Rb6	Bc8			
12.	a4	f5	24.	Ne2	f4			

GAME 84

1.	e4	e6	17.	Re3	O-O-O	33.	f3	Bd7
2.	d4	d5	18.	Rg3	Kb8	34.	a5	Kc7
3.	Nc3	Bb4	19.	Rf3	f5	35.	Kf2	Rf7
4.	e5	c5	20.	exf6	e5	36.	Ke3	Kd6
5.	a3	Bxc3+	21.	Qg3	Nxd4	37.	g3	Kc5
6.	bxc3	Qc7	22.	Re3	e4	38.	f4	Bg4
7.	Nf3	Nc6	23.	Rxe4	Qxg3	39.	Rb1	Re7+
8.	Be2	Bd7	24.	Rxd4	Qg4	40.	Kd2	b6
9.	O-O	Nge7	25.	Rxg4	Bxg4	41.	axb6	axb6
10.	a4	Na5	26.	Bxg6	Rhg8	42.	h3	Bd7
11.	Re1	cxd4	27.	Bh7	Rh8	43.	g4	d4
12.	cxd4	Nc4	28.	Bd3	Rde8	44.	f5	Re3
13.	Bd3	h6	29.	f7	Re7	45.	f6	Rf3
14.	Nd2	Nxd2	30.	f8/Q+	RxQ	46.	Rf1	Rxf1
15.	Bxd2	Nc6	31.	Bb4	Rff7	47.	Bxf1	Be6
16.	Qg4	g6	32.	Bxe7	Rxe7		(1–0)	

GAME 85

1.	e4	c5	19.	Bg5	Qxd1+	37.	Bg5	Bxg5+
2.	Nf3	d6	20.	Rxd1	Rfe8	38.	hxg5	Kg7
3.	c3	Nf6	21.	Bb3	c4	39.	Ke3	Kg6
4.	Bd3	Nc6	22.	Bc2	Ne6	40.	Kf4	Nc5
5.	Bc2	Bg4	23.	Be3	Reb8	41.	g3	Bd7
6.	d3	g6	24.	Rb1	a6	42.	a3	Be8
7.	Nbd2	Bg7	25.	Rff1	Be8	43.	Bb1	Na4
8.	h3	Bd7	26.	Kf2	Nd8	44.	Ne2	Nb2
9.	O-O	O-O	27.	Rxb8	Rxb8	45.	Nd4	Nd1
10.	Nh2	b5	28.	Rb1	Rb5	46.	Ne2	Nf2
11.	f4	b4	29.	Rxb5	axb5	47.	Ke3	Nh3
12.	Nc4	d5	30.	Ke2	h6	48.	Nf4+	Kxg5
13.	Ne5	bxc3	31.	Kd2	g5	49.	Ng2	f6
14.	bxc3	dxe4	32.	h4	g4	50.	exf6	Kxf6
15.	dxe4	Nxe5	33.	Nd4	e6	51.	Nh4	e5
16.	fxe5	Ne8	34.	Bf4	h5	52.	Bc2	Bd7
17.	Nf3	Nc7	35.	Bg5	Nb7	53.	Bb1	Ng5
18.	Rf2	Bb5	36.	Bf6	Bh6+	54.	Bc2	Nf7

55. Bb1	Nh8	**62.** Kh2	Ke7	**69.** Kg1	Bxe4
56. Bc2	Ng6	**63.** Kg1	Kd6	**70.** Bxe4	Ka4
57. Nxg6	Kxg6	**64.** Kf2	Kc5	**71.** Bf5	Kb3
58. Kf2	Kg5	**65.** Kg1	Kb6	**72.** Bxg4	e4
59. Kg2	h4	**66.** Kh1	Ka5	**73.** Bxh3	Kxc3
60. Kh2	h3	**67.** Kg1	Bc6	**74.** g4	Kd2
61. Kg1	Kf6	**68.** Kh1	Bb7	(0–1)	

GAME 86

1. e4	g6	**.9.** O-O-O	Ne7	**17.** fxe6	fxe6
2. d4	Bg7	**10.** g4	Qa5	**18.** Bc4	Nxe5
3. Nc3	d6	**11.** Kb1	Rb8	**19.** Qg3	Bg7
4. f4	c6	**12.** e5	dxe5	**20.** Bxd5	cxd5
5. Nf3	Bg4	**13.** dxe5	Nd5	**21.** Bh6	Qc7
6. Be3	Nd7	**14.** Ne4	Bf8	**22.** Nd6+	Kd8
7. h3	Bxf3	**15.** Bc1	b5	**23.** Bxg7	Qxd6
8. Qxf3	e6	**16.** f5	b4	**24.** Qxe5	(1–0)

GAME 87

1. d4	Nf6	**10.** Nxc4	Nbd7	**19.** e5	dxe5
2. Nf3	c5	**11.** Re1	Ba6	**20.** fxe5	Nxd5
3. d5	b5	**12.** Qa4	Qc8	**21.** Nxd5	Qxc6
4. c4	Bb7	**13.** Na5	Nb6	**22.** e6	Ne5
5. g3	g6	**14.** Qh4	Re8	**23.** Rxe5	Bxe5
6. Bg2	bxc4	**15.** Bg5	Qc7	**24.** exf7	Rf8
7. Nc3	Bg7	**16.** Nc6	Bb7	**25.** h3	Rxf7
8. O-O	O-O	**17.** e4	Nbd7	♟ **26.** Nf4	Rxf4
9. Ne5	d6	**18.** f4	Kh8	(0–1)	

GAME 88

1. e4	e6	**16.** Ng5	h6	**31.** h3	Rc8
2. d4	d5	**17.** Ne4	Nxe4	**32.** Kf1	Ra8
3. Nc3	Nf6	**18.** Rxe4	Qd6	**33.** Kg1	a5
4. Bg5	dxe4	**19.** Qh5	c5	**34.** Qe4	Rd8
5. Nxe4	Be7	**20.** Rg4	Kf8	**35.** Rg3	Kf7
6. Bxf6	Bxf6	**21.** Rd3	cxd4	**36.** Qh7	Rg8
7. Nf3	Nbd7	**22.** Rgxd4	Qc7	**37.** Qg6+	Ke7
8. Bc4	O-O	**23.** Qh4	Rxd4	**38.** Qxg7+	Rxg7
9. O-O	c6	**24.** Qxd4	Re8	**39.** Rxg7+	Kd6
10. Qe2	b6	**25.** Bb5	Bc6	**40.** Rxc7	Kxc7
11. Rad1	Qc7	**26.** a4	Bxb5	**41.** g4	Kd6
12. Nxf6+	Nxf6	**27.** axb5	f6	**42.** h4	e5
13. Qe5	Qe7	**28.** c4	Rc8	**43.** g5	(1–0)
14. c3	Bb7	**29.** b3	Re8		
15. Rfe1	Rfd8	**30.** f4	Ke7		

GAME 89

1. e4	c5	9. f4	Nc6	17. Bxc6	Rxc6
2. Nf3	d6	10. Nxc6	Bxc6	18. Rad1	Rfc8
3. d4	cxd4	11. f5	e5	19. Nd5	Qd8
4. Nxd4	Nf6	12. Qd3	Be7	20. c3	Be7
5. Nc3	a6	13. Bg5	Qb6+	21. Ra1	f6
6. Bc4	e6	14. Kh1	O-O	22. a4	Rb8
7. Bb3	b5	15. Bxf6	Bxf6	23. Nxe7+	(1–0)
8. O-O	Bb7	16. Bd5	Rac8		

GAME 90

1. e4	c5	9. c4	bxc4	17. Nf5+	Ke8
2. Nf3	d6	10. Bxc4	Bxe4	18. Be3	Bxe3
3. d4	cxd4	11. O-O	d5	19. fxe3	Qb6
4. Nxd4	Nf6	12. Re1	e5	20. Rd1	Ra7
5. Nc3	a6	13. Qa4+	Nd7	21. Rd6	Qd8
6. h3	b5	14. Rxe4	dxe4	22. Qb3	Qc7
7. Nd5	Bb7	15. Nf5	Bc5	23. Bxf7+	Kd8
8. Nxf6+	gxf6	16. Ng7+	Ke7	24. Be6	(1–0)

GAME 91

1. e4	c5	15. Nd5	Nc6	29. Bb3	f5
2. Nf3	Nc6	16. Ne3	Qc5	30. g3	Re8
3. d4	cxd4	17. c3	Rad8	31. Qc6	Qb8
4. Nxd4	Nf6	18. Qf3	Rd7	32. Rd7	Re1+
5. Nc3	d6	19. Rad1	Rd6	33. Kf2	Qe8
6. Bg5	g6	20. Rxd6	Qxd6	34. Qf3	Rb1
7. Bxf6	exf6	21. Rd1	Qc5	35. Rd1	Rxb2+
8. Bc4	Bg7	22. h3	b5	36. Kg1	Qc8
9. O-O	O-O	23. Rd5	Qb6	37. h4	Bxc3
10. Ndb5	f5	24. Rd6	Ne5	38. Rd8+	Qxd8
11. exf5	Bxf5	25. Qd5	Qc7	39. Qxc3+	Qf6
12. Nxd6	Ne5	26. f4	Nc4	40. Qxf6 mate	(1–0)
13. Bb3	Qd7	27. Nxc4	bxc4		
14. Nxf5	Qxf5	28. Bxc4	Kh8		

GAME 92

1. Nf3	Nf6	8. e4	Nbd7	15. Bc4	Nxc3
2. c4	g6	9. Rd1	Nb6	16. Bc5	Rfe8+
3. Nc3	Bg7	10. Qc5	Bg4	17. Kf1	Be6
4. d4	O-O	11. Bg5	Na4	18. Bxb6	Bxc4+
5. Bf4	d5	12. Qa3	Nxc3	19. Kg1	Ne2+
6. Qb3	dxc4	13. bxc3	Nxe4	20. Kf1	Nxd4+
7. Qxc4	c6	14. Bxe7	Qb6	21. Kg1	Ne2+

22.	Kf1	Nc3+	29.	Qd8+	Bf8	36.	Kf1	Ng3+
23.	Kg1	axb6	30.	Nxe1	Bd5	37.	Ke1	Bb4+
24.	Qb4	Ra4	31.	Nf3	Ne4	38.	Kd1	Bb3+
25.	Qxb6	Nxd1	32.	Qb8	b5	39.	Kc1	Ne2+
26.	h3	Rxa2	33.	h4	h5	40.	Kb1	Nc3+
27.	Kh2	Nxf2	34.	Ne5	Kg7	41.	Kc1	Rc2 mate
28.	Re1	Rxe1	35.	Kg1	Bc5+		(0–1)	

GAME 93

1.	e4	c5	17.	Nf6+	Bxf6	33.	Rde7+	Kd8
2.	Nf3	Nc6	18.	Qxf6	Qc7	34.	Rd7+	Kc8
3.	d4	cxd4	19.	O-O-O	Rxa2	35.	Rc7+	Kd8
4.	Nxd4	e6	20.	Kb1	Ra6	36.	Rfd7+	Ke8
5.	Nc3	Qc7	21.	Bxb5	Rb6	37.	Rd1	b5
6.	g3	Nf6	22.	Bd3	e5	38.	Rb7	Qh5
7.	Ndb5	Qb8	23.	fxe5	Rxf6	39.	g4	Qh3
8.	Bf4	Ne5	24.	exf6	Qc5	40.	g5	Qf3
9.	Be2	Bc5	25.	Bxh7	Qg5	41.	Re1+	Kf8
10.	Bxe5	Qxe5	26.	Bxg8	Qxf6	42.	Rxb5	Kg7
11.	f4	Qb8	27.	Rhf1	Qxg7	43.	Rb6	Qg3
12.	e5	a6	28.	Bxf7+	Kd8	44.	Rd1	Qc7
13.	exf6	axb5	29.	Be6	Qh6	45.	Rdd6	Qc8
14.	fxg7	Rg8	30.	Bxd7	Bxd7	46.	b3	Kh7
15.	Ne4	Be7	31.	Rf7	Qxh2	47.	Ra6	(1–0)
16.	Qd4	Ra4	32.	Rdxd7+	Ke8			

GAME 94

1.	e4	e5	7.	O-O	dxc3	13.	Bb2	Qg5
2.	Nf3	Nc6	8.	Qb3	Qe7	14.	h4	Qxh4
3.	Bc4	Bc5	9.	Nxc3	Nf6	15.	Bxg7	Rg8
4.	b4	Bxb4	10.	Nd5	Nxd5	16.	Rfe1+	Kd8
5.	c3	Ba5	11.	exd5	Ne5	17.	Qg3	(1–0)
6.	d4	exd4	12.	Nxe5	Qxe5			

GAME 95

1.	e4	e6	13.	Ne2	O-O-O	25.	h6	Qd6
2.	d4	d5	14.	c4	e5	26.	Qg5+	Qe7
3.	Nc3	Bb4	15.	dxe5	Nxe5	27.	Qd5+	Qd6
4.	a3	Bxc3+	16.	Rxd8+	Kxd8	28.	Qg5+	Qe7
5.	bxc3	dxe4	17.	Nf4	Rg8	29.	Qg3	Bf5
6.	Qg4	Nf6	18.	Be2	Kc8	30.	Qf4	Qe6
7.	Qxg7	Rg8	19.	Rd1	Rd8	31.	g4	Bg6
8.	Qh6	Rg6	20.	Rxd8+	Kxd8	32.	Qg5+	Qe7
9.	Qe3	b6	21.	Qg3	Ng6	33.	Qd5+	Qd6
10.	Bb2	Bb7	22.	h4	Nxf4	34.	Be5	Qxd5
11.	O-O-O	Nbd7	23.	Qxf4	Ne8	35.	cxd5	f6
12.	h3	Qe7	24.	h5	Bc8	36.	Bg3	Ke7

37. Kd2	Nd6	43. Ba2	f5	49. Bg6	Bd7
38. Ke3	b5	44. gxf5	Bxf5	50. Bxh7	c5
39. Bxd6 +	Kxd6	45. Bb3	Bg6	51. dxc6	Bxc6
40. Kd4	a6	46. Ba4	Bf5	52. Bxe4	Bxe4
41. c4	bxc4	47. Be8	Ke7	53. Kxe4	Kf6
42. Bxc4	a5	48. Ke5	Bg4	54. f4	(1–0)

GAME 96

1. e4	e5	10. Rd1	O-O	19. Rxd5	Bxc3
2. Nf3	Nc6	11. c4	bxc4	20. Rc1	Bb4
3. Bb5	a6	12. Bxc4	Qd7	21. Rxc7	Rac8
4. Ba4	Nf6	13. Nc3	Nxc3	22. Ra7	Rc2
5. O-O	Nxe4	14. bxc3	f6	23. Rdd7	Bc3
6. d4	b5	15. exf6	Bxf6	24. Rac7	h6
7. Bb3	d5	16. Bg5	Na5	25. Be3	(1–0)
8. dxe5	Be6	17. Qxe6 +	Qxe6		
9. Qe2	Be7	18. Bxd5	Qxd5		

GAME 97

1. d4	Nf6	15. b3	Qc7	29. Rd1	Qxc3
2. c4	g6	16. f4	b5	30. Bxc3	Nxd1
3. Nc3	Bg7	17. cxb5	Qb6	31. Qd4	Nxc3
4. Nf3	O-O	18. Kh2	axb5	32. b6	Rc5
5. Bf4	c5	19. Nxb5	Bxa1	33. e5	Rxa4
6. d5	d6	20. Rxa1	Rfc8	34. b7	Rxd4
7. e4	Qa5	21. Qc4	Qa6	35. b8/Q +	Kg7
8. Bd3	Bg4	22. a4	Nb6	36. exd6	exd6
9. O-O	Nbd7	23. Qc2	c4	37. Qxd6	Rcxd6
10. h3	Bxf3	24. b4	c3	38. Qc7	Ne2
11. Qxf3	Ne5	25. Nxc3	Qc4.	39. f5	Rxf5
12. Qe2	Nxd3	26. b5	Qd4	40. Qa7	Rfd5
13. Qxd3	a6	27. Be1	Nc4	41. Qa8	Nf4
14. Bd2	Nd7	28. Qf2	Ne3	(0–1)	

GAME 98

1. e4	c5	15. Be3	a6	29. Rd1	Qf6
2. Nf3	Nc6	16. Nc3	Nxe4	30. Rxd8 +	Qxd8
3. d4	cxd4	17. Rxf7	Rxf7	31. Bxa6	Qd5
4. Nxd4	Nf6	18. Bxf7 +	Kh8	32. a3	h5
5. Nc3	d6	19. Qc4	Bg5	33. b4	Qd1 +
6. Bc4	e6	20. Nxe4	Bxe3 +	34. Kh2	h4
7. Bb3	Be7	21. Kh1	Qd7	35. Qf4	Qe1
8. O-O	O-O	22. Bh5	Bb5	36. b5	Bd5
9. Be3	Bd7	23. Qb3	Qd4	37. b6	e3
10. f4	Nxd4	24. Nd6	Qxd6	38. b7	Bxb7
11. Bxd4	Bc6	25. Qxe3	Bc6	39. Qf8 +	Kh7
12. Qe2	b5	26. Bf3	e4	40. Bd3 +	g6
13. Nxb5	e5	27. Be2	Rd8	41. Qf7 +	Kh8
14. fxe5	dxe5	28. h3	h6	42. Qxg6	(1–0)

GAME 99

1. e4	c5	7. Bb3	a6	13. f5	Qb4
2. Nf3	d6	8. f4	Qa5	14. fxe6	Bxe6
3. d4	cxd4	9. O-O	Nxd4	15. Bxe6	fxe6
4. Nxd4	Nf6	10. Qxd4	d5	16. Rxf8 +	Qxf8
5. Nc3	Nc6	11. Be3	Nxe4	17. Qa4 +	(1–0)
6. Bc4	e6	12. Nxe4	dxe4		

GAME 100

1. e4	c5	15. Bf4	Nc4	29. Rxd6	Bf5
2. Nf3	Nc6	16. Qe2	Bxf4	30. b4	Rff8
3. d4	cxd4	17. Qxc4	Kg7	31. b5	Nd8
4. Nxd4	g6	18. Ne4	Bc7	32. Rd5	Nf7
5. Nc3	Bg7	19. Nc5	Rf6	33. Rc5	a6
6. Be3	Nf6	20. c3	e5	34. b6	Be4
7. Bc4	O-O	21. Rad1	Nd8	35. Re1	Bc6
8. Bb3	Na5	22. Nd7	Rc6	36. Rxc6	bxc6
9. e5	Ne8	23. Qh4	Re6	37. b7	Rab8
10. Bxf7 +	Kxf7	24. Nc5	Rf6	38. Qxa6	Nd8
11. Ne6	dxe6	25. Ne4	Rf4	39. Rb1	Rf7
12. Qxd8	Nc6	26. Qxe7 +	Rf7	40. h3	Rfxb7
13. Qd2	Bxe5	27. Qa3	Nc6	41. Rxb7	Rxb7
14. O-O	Nd6	28. Nd6	Bxd6	42. Qa8	(1–0)

GAME 101

1. d4	Nf6	13. Qc2	Qc6	25. e5	R6d7
2. c4	b6	14. Bd3	Qxc2	26. Nc1	Bf8
3. Nc3	Bb7	15. Bxc2	O-O-O	27. b4	Nc4
4. f3	d5	16. Kf2	Rd6	28. Ra2	Nxe5
5. cxd5	Nxd5	17. b3	Nc6	29. Rc2	b5
6. Nxd5	Qxd5	18. Rd2	Rhd8	30. Ne2	Nc4
7. e4	Qd7	19. Rhd1	Nb4	31. Rc3	e5
8. Bc4	g6	20. Bb1	Ba6	32. f4	exd4
9. Qb3	e6	21. a3	Nc6	33. Rxd4	Nxe3
10. Ne2	Bg7	22. Bd3	Bxd3	34. Kxe3	Rxd4
11. Be3	Nc6	23. Rxd3	f5	35. Nxd4	Rxd4
12. Rd1	Na5	24. R3d2	Na5	(0–1)	

About the Author

Bruce Pandolfini, a U.S. National Chess Master, gained prominence as an analyst on PBS's live telecast of the Fischer-Spassky championship match in 1972. In due course, he lectured widely on chess and in 1978 was chosen to deliver the Bobby Fischer Chess Lectures at the University of Alabama in Birmingham. His first book, *Let's Play Chess*, appeared in 1980. The author is a *Chess Life* magazine consulting editor, for which he writes the monthly "ABCs of Chess." He has also written columns for *Time-Video*, the *Litchfield County Times*, and *Physician's Travel and Meeting Guide*.

As a chess teacher, he's been on the faculty of the New School for Social Research since 1973, and currently conducts chess classes at Browning, Trinity, and the Little Red School House in New York City. With U.S. Champion Lev Alburt, he has developed special children's programs sponsored by the American Chess Foundation. The director of the world famous Manhattan Chess Club at Carnegie Hall, Pandolfini visited the USSR in the fall of 1984 to study their teaching methods and observe the controversial championship match between Anatoly Karpov and Gary Kasparov.